Raising
Healthy
Children
Day by Day

**366 Readings
for Parents,
Teachers, and
Caregivers**

Birth to Age 5

Jolene L. Roehlkepartain

free spirit
PUBLISHING®

Works
for kids®

Library of Congress Cataloging-in-Publication Data
Roehlkepartain, Jolene L., 1962–
    Raising healthy children day by day: 366 readings for parents, teachers, and care-givers, birth to age 5 / by Jolene L. Roehlkepartain.
        p. cm.
    Includes indexes.
    ISBN 1-57542-094-5 (pbk.)
    1. Child rearing—Miscellanea. 2. Parenting—Miscellanea. 3. Parent and child—Miscellanea. 4. Children and adults—Miscellanea. 5. Conduct of life. 6. Affirmations. I. Title.

HQ769 .R6174 2001
649'.1—dc21   00-053571

At the time of this book's publication, all facts and figures cited are the most current available; all telephone numbers, addresses, and Web site URLs are accurate and active; all publications, organizations, Web sites, and other resources exist as described in this book; and all have been verified. The author and Free Spirit Publishing make no warranty or guarantee concerning the information and materials given out by organizations or content found at Web sites, and we are not responsible for any changes that occur after this book's publication. If you find an error or believe that a resource listed here is not as described, please contact Free Spirit Publishing. Parents, teachers, and other adults: We strongly urge you to monitor children's use of the Internet.

The framework of developmental assets that is the basis for this book is used under a license from Search Institute, 700 S. Third St., Suite 210, Minneapolis, MN 55415. Copyright © 1997 by Search Institute. For more information, visit the Web site (*www.search-institute.org*).

Edited by Elizabeth Verdick and KaTrina Wentzel
Cover and book design by Marieka Heinlen

10 9 8 7 6 5 4 3 2 1
Printed in the
United States of America

Free Spirit Publishing Inc.
217 Fifth Avenue North, Suite 200
Minneapolis, MN 55401-1299
(612) 338-2068
help4kids@freespirit.com
www.freespirit.com

The following are registered trademarks
of Free Spirit Publishing Inc.:

FREE SPIRIT®
FREE SPIRIT PUBLISHING®
SELF-HELP FOR TEENS®
SELF-HELP FOR KIDS®
WORKS FOR KIDS®
THE FREE SPIRITED CLASSROOM®

free spirit
PUBLISHING®
Works
for kids®

To Linnea,
who brings me much joy

Contents

Introduction

When tucking their toddler into bed at night, a mom and dad play a game called "I love you bigger than . . . " Taking turns, the parents and their young son come up with bigger and better ways to fill in the final phrase.

***

A two-year-old boy shakes a rattle at his five-month-old sister. "Want to play?" he asks. She reaches for the rattle, shakes it, and smiles. Her brother lovingly grins back at her.

***

A three-year-old girl falls down outside while playing with a classmate. Her teacher rushes over to soothe her. The classmate begins crying, too, and reaches out to hold the injured girl's hand. The teacher comforts both girls until they're ready to play again.

We can't help but admire the parents, the older brother, the teacher, and the sensitive classmate who cries on behalf of her friend and tries to comfort her. We're filled with warm feelings when we see adults and young children interacting in loving, caring ways. As parents,* teachers, and caregivers, these are the experiences we want to give our children.

Since 1989, Search Institute—a Minneapolis-based organization specializing in research on children and teenagers—has been studying what helps children grow up to be caring, healthy, and productive adults. After surveying communities across the country and reviewing the responses of almost 100,000 young people in grades six through twelve, the researchers identified forty key factors that make a powerful difference in the lives of children and teenagers. Search Institute calls these factors *developmental assets.* They include, among others, family support, safety, creative activities, reading for pleasure, peaceful conflict resolution, and self-esteem.

While the research has focused on young people in grades six through twelve, Search Institute has created lists of the forty assets for four additional age groups: **infants** (birth to twelve months), **toddlers** (thirteen to thirty-five months), **preschoolers**

---

*Throughout the book, the word *parent* refers to children's primary caregivers. Of course, not all children live with two biological parents, or even one. But rather than list all the possibilities (guardians, stepparents, foster parents, grandparents, etc.), the word *parent* is used to keep things simple. If you're an adult who's caring for a child, parent means *you.*

(ages three to five), and **elementary-age children** (ages six to eleven). *Raising Healthy Children Day by Day* is about developing these assets in children ages birth to five.

Why are the developmental assets important? Because Search Institute researchers discovered that the more assets young people have, the more likely they are to be caring, competent, contributing members of their community. The researchers also have found that the more assets young people have, the less likely they are to get into trouble or lose their way as they grow up.

For example, the researchers determined that sixth graders who have more assets are less likely to hit someone, smoke cigarettes, shoplift, get depressed, or ride with a drunk driver. They're also more likely to help others, resist danger, succeed in school, and not give up when life gets difficult. These are the things we want for *all* children—young children included. The forty developmental assets give parents, teachers, and caregivers practical ways to help children of all ages to grow up well.

The developmental assets are grouped into eight categories to help simplify them. The following pages list all forty assets and the eight categories they fall into.

Support Assets

#1: FAMILY SUPPORT
#2: POSITIVE FAMILY COMMUNICATION
#3: OTHER ADULT RELATIONSHIPS
#4: CARING NEIGHBORHOOD
#5: CARING OUT-OF-HOME CLIMATE
#6: PARENT INVOLVEMENT IN OUT-OF-HOME SITUATIONS

Empowerment Assets

#7: COMMUNITY VALUES CHILDREN
#8: CHILDREN ARE GIVEN USEFUL ROLES
#9: SERVICE TO OTHERS
#10: SAFETY

Boundaries and Expectations Assets

#11: FAMILY BOUNDARIES
#12: OUT-OF-HOME BOUNDARIES
#13: NEIGHBORHOOD BOUNDARIES
#14: ADULT ROLE MODELS
#15: POSITIVE PEER INTERACTION AND INFLUENCE
#16: APPROPRIATE EXPECTATIONS FOR GROWTH

Constructive Use of Time Assets

#17: CREATIVE ACTIVITIES
#18: OUT-OF-HOME ACTIVITIES
#19: RELIGIOUS COMMUNITY
#20: POSITIVE, SUPERVISED TIME AT HOME

Commitment to Learning Assets

#21: ACHIEVEMENT EXPECTATION AND MOTIVATION
#22: CHILDREN ARE ENGAGED IN LEARNING
#23: STIMULATING ACTIVITY AND HOMEWORK
#24: ENJOYMENT OF LEARNING AND BONDING TO SCHOOL
#25: READING FOR PLEASURE

Positive Values Assets

#26: FAMILY VALUES CARING
#27: FAMILY VALUES EQUALITY AND SOCIAL JUSTICE
#28: FAMILY VALUES INTEGRITY
#29: FAMILY VALUES HONESTY
#30: FAMILY VALUES RESPONSIBILITY
#31: FAMILY VALUES HEALTHY LIFESTYLE

Social Competencies Assets

#32: PLANNING AND DECISION MAKING
#33: INTERPERSONAL SKILLS
#34: CULTURAL COMPETENCE
#35: RESISTANCE SKILLS
#36: PEACEFUL CONFLICT RESOLUTION

Positive Identity Assets

#37: PERSONAL POWER
#38: SELF-ESTEEM
#39: SENSE OF PURPOSE
#40: POSITIVE VIEW OF PERSONAL FUTURE

Children go through many changes between infancy and the preschool years, so Search Institute has drafted language for each asset for each age group. You might find it helpful to look first at the general asset names on the previous pages, and then turn to the specific definitions most relevant to the ages of the children in your care. On pages 367–373, you'll find specific asset definitions for infants. Pages 373–379 list the asset definitions for toddlers. And pages 379–385 list them for preschoolers. We invite you to copy these definitions to hang in your home, classroom, or childcare center, or to carry with you. This way, you'll always be reminded of your role as an asset builder.

About This Book

Raising Healthy Children Day by Day is a book of daily readings, meaning there's a page for every day of the year (including February 29 for Leap Year). Each reading begins with a *quotation* meant to get you interested and start you thinking. A brief *essay* goes deeper into the topic. You might find questions to consider, tips to try, examples, or a story related to the quotation. An *I-statement* suggests an action you might take, a decision you might make, or another way to use these ideas to support young children in your everyday life.

As you'll see, some of the daily readings focus specifically on infants, toddlers, or preschoolers.

Other readings apply to all three age groups. Some readings speak mainly to parents, while others are directed toward teachers or caregivers. If you're a parent of an infant, we encourage you to read entries about toddlers and preschoolers, so you're more prepared as your child grows. If you're a teacher or caregiver, you may also be a parent—and so the readings may apply to you at home and away from home. Even if a reading doesn't fit your specific situation at home, at school, or in your childcare center, it can still have value to you. One of the most important messages of this book is that *all of us* are responsible for young children—those in our homes, our schools, our childcare centers, our communities, and in the broader world. We can all do our part to meet children's physical and emotional needs and help them grow up in warm, caring, supportive environments.

At the end of each daily reading, you'll find words that tie in to a specific developmental asset. They may look like this:

EMPOWERMENT
ASSET #8: CHILDREN ARE GIVEN USEFUL ROLES

or this:

POSITIVE VALUES
ASSET #26: FAMILY VALUES CARING

After reading the quote, essay, I-statement, and asset for any given day, you may wish to refer to the specific definition for the asset as it applies to the ages of the children in your family, classroom, or childcare center. Yet, whether you're aware that you're building a specific asset isn't important— what's important is that each daily reading is based on a research framework that shows adults how to raise healthy children day by day.

This is *your* book. Use it any way you want. The easiest and most obvious is to turn to today's date and read its entry at the start of the day. Think about what you've read and try out the I-statement. If you'd rather read it before you go to bed at night, read the next day's entry and sleep on it. If you want to share the book with others, you might use it as part of a parent group, a childcare provider meeting, or a preschool training. If you want to use it as a way to learn more about each individual asset, do that. If you simply want to get an idea for how to bring out the best in a young child, read the day's entry with that purpose in mind.

If you'd like to learn more about Search Institute's continuing work on developmental assets for children, visit their Web site *(www.search-institute.org)*. Or check out the book *What Young Children Need to Succeed: Working Together to Build Assets from Birth to Age 11* (Free Spirit Publishing, 2000), which includes more than 1,000 practical ideas for building assets in infants, toddlers, preschoolers, and elementary-age children.

If you have questions, success stories, or further ideas for building assets in young children, we'd love to hear from you. You can write to this address:

Raising Healthy Children Day by Day
c/o Free Spirit Publishing Inc.
217 Fifth Avenue North, Suite 200
Minneapolis, MN 55401-1299

Or send an email:
help4kids@freespirit.com

You can also visit Free Spirit online:
www.freespirit.com

January 1

**"The best thing about the future
is that it comes one day at a time."**
Abraham Lincoln

Sometimes we make New Year's resolutions for children: This year, Mara will learn to use the potty. Luis will adjust to his bedtime routine. Alisa will stop sucking her thumb. While these are worthwhile goals, we may push children to achieve them according to a deadline that meets *our* needs, not theirs. Children feel more secure when they have a sense of control over their lives. To build on children's success, honor the progress they've already made and affirm each small step they take. By this time next year, you'll see how far they've come.

Today
I'll accept that children grow at their own pace.

January 2

**"Language skills are essential . . .
everything else flows from that."**
Linda Marsa

Long before they start to speak, children learn
about communicating. Infants watch how we talk
and listen to sounds we make. By four months,
babies begin to babble. Children usually know
about 300 words by age three, 1,500 words by age
four, and 2,500 words by age five. You boost their
language development when you read to them or
teach songs and finger plays. When communicating with children, hold them on your lap or kneel
down to look them in the eye as you speak. This
reinforces the message that your words—and
theirs—are important.

Today
I'll have a face-to-face conversation with my child.

January 3

"Niyimpa kor ntsetse ba."
"It takes an entire village to raise a child."
Benin proverb

Parents play the primary role in raising their children, but many other people within a community have a major impact, too. Educator and parent Lynn Stambaugh made a list of all of the adults who regularly interacted with her children—not just teachers and childcare providers, but also neighbors, custodians, bus drivers, and others. Then she wrote each one a letter, thanking him or her for making a difference in her children's lives. Many of the recipients wrote or phoned her back to thank her for her appreciation—and became even more involved as a result.

Today
I'll list the adults in my child's life.

January 4

"Learn to see and so avoid all danger."
Buddha

Most of us realize the danger of children getting into cleaning products. But what about other household items? According to the American Association of Poison Control Centers, four major sources of poisonings are: (1) cosmetics and personal care products, (2) pain relievers, (3) plants, and (4) foreign objects, such as small batteries, toy parts, buttons, or coins. Are the areas where your child lives and plays fully childproofed? Experts recommend getting on your hands and knees to view rooms at a child's eye level. You may be surprised by what you see.

Today
I'll do a safety check.

EMPOWERMENT
ASSET #10: SAFETY

January 5

"Adults need children in their lives to listen to and care for, to keep their imagination fresh and their hearts young."
Margaret Mead

When you were a child, was there an adult you admired who took the time to talk with you? Someone who lit up in your presence—and lit up something deep inside you? If so, this person gave you a gift. You can give this gift, too—even if you never had someone like this in your life—by becoming a child's role model. Take time now to connect with a child, especially one in need of support. You'll rediscover how it feels to be young, and you'll make a difference as an adult.

Today

I'll spend one-on-one time with a child.

January 6

"Donde hay voluntad, hay modo."
"Where there's a will, there's a way."
Southwestern Spanish proverb

As adults, we're motivated when we do something that stimulates us — work, a hobby, service to others, time with family and friends. Children are often motivated by curiosity. They love to explore — to discover more about themselves and the world: *Who's that in the mirror? How can these puzzle pieces fit? What happens when sand is mixed with water? Why do dogs like to lick faces?* Nurture this motivation to foster a lifelong love of learning. (And forget that old saying "Curiosity killed the cat.")

Today
I'll encourage a child to explore.

January 7

**"Learning to interact successfully
with other children is a process."**
Claire Lerner

Young children are just beginning to learn how to
talk, play, and get along with others. It may take
years of practice for a child to develop these social
skills. You can gently guide children by modeling
manners and ways to communicate with respect.
Point out how good it feels to say something kind,
lend a helping hand, or give a hug. Teach children
the words they can use: "Please." "Thank you." "It's
your turn now." "I need help." In time, they'll follow your lead.

Today
I'll model respectful communication.

January 8

**"I feel everyone has a song inside.
It's a matter of whether it can be brought out."**
June Kuramoto

For adults and children alike, music is a source of pleasure. It provides a link to our emotions—and to each other. For young children, music has the added benefit of enhancing creativity and language skills. If you're the parent or caregiver of an infant, remember the power of singing to and with your child throughout the day and into the night. Learn and sing the songs from various cultures and traditions to expose your baby to different sounds and rhythms. You can play soothing lullabies or even record yourself singing, so your child can listen while falling asleep.

Today
I'll sing to my baby.

CONSTRUCTIVE USE OF TIME
ASSET #17: CREATIVE ACTIVITIES

January 9

"Teach children how to see themselves accurately,
so that when problems are their fault,
they take responsibility
and try to correct their behavior."
Martin E. P. Seligman, Ph.D.

Do your kids play the "blame game"? Do you often hear, "He *made* me do it" or "It's all *her* fault"? Children may even blame the furniture if they stub their toes! Teach children to recognize and understand their part in what happened. Let them know that blaming others makes things worse, not better. You might say, "I'm not happy that you broke the lamp, but I'm glad that you told me about it. How can you be more careful next time?" Even very young children can accept and learn from their mistakes.

Today
I'll help my children take responsibility.

January 10

"Your success depends mainly upon what you think of yourself and whether you believe in yourself."
William J. H. Boetcker

You know how proud and pleased you feel when you achieve something you've worked toward. Young children also take pleasure in their own successes—big and small. From birth to age five, children are forming beliefs about their self-worth. Infants respond to and return the smiles and coos of their parents; toddlers feel proud when they build with blocks or scribble with crayons; preschoolers love to show off new skills like doing somersaults or putting on a shirt without help. Each accomplishment raises children's self-esteem. And children feel valued when you affirm their success.

Today
I'll applaud children's efforts.

POSITIVE IDENTITY
ASSET #38: SELF-ESTEEM

January 11

**"It takes everybody to create
the best possible childcare."**
Betty Holcomb

The National Association for the Education of Young Children (NAEYC) guidelines recommend that care facilities for infants, toddlers, and preschoolers have a certain caregiver-to-child ratio: one adult for every three to four infants, one adult for every four to six toddlers, one adult for every seven to ten preschoolers. This allows caregivers to offer young children more individual attention and better serve their needs. Only six states follow the NAEYC guidelines (Alabama, Connecticut, Hawaii, Oregon, Pennsylvania, and Rhode Island). If you live in one of the other forty-four states, you can contact your legislator to advocate for consistent state standards. This is a great way to show your support for young children.

Today
**I'll advocate for NAEYC standards
in my childcare center or state.**

January 12

"It takes a lot of courage to show your dreams to someone else."
Erma Bombeck

Part of giving children support is taking them seriously. When a young child announces that he or she has superhuman strength or will someday catch a whale and ride on its back, it's tempting to laugh or say, "Isn't that cute?" But if children feel that you're making fun of their dreams and fantasies, they may be less likely to share them with you. So show interest, keep eye contact, ask follow-up questions, and search out resources for children. They'll see that you care and that you're a willing listener.

Today
I'll support a young child's aspirations.

January 13

**"A faith community can provide
a special quality of nurture."**
Jean Grasso Fitzpatrick

Many families have found that their faith community offers a chance for their infants and young children to interact with caring adults outside the
home. Faith communities provide other social benefits as well: children can find friends, families can
meet and develop networks of support, and senior
citizens can connect with people from different generations. In fact, a religious community can support
and nurture every member of your family. If you
aren't already part of a faith community or if you
haven't been to your place of worship for a while,
you may want to think about joining—or rejoin-
ing—for your children and for yourself.

Today
I'll consider the benefits of a faith community.

January 14

"Time is the ultimate scarce resource we have."
Mihaly Csikszentmihalyi, Ph.D.

These days, our time is scarce. Many of us are busier than ever, but our children still need us. Show young children the importance of planning ahead and making time for things that matter most. Together, arrange a play date for you and your preschooler. Invite your toddler to help you make cookies or prepare a healthy snack. Or let the dishes sit, so you can sing to your infant. These activities add up to time well spent—for you and your child.

Today
I'll set aside time for my child.

SOCIAL COMPETENCIES
ASSET #32: PLANNING AND DECISION MAKING

January 15

*"The ultimate measure of a man
is not where he stands in moments
of comfort and convenience, but where he stands
at times of challenge and controversy."*
Martin Luther King Jr.

Today is the birth anniversary of Martin Luther King Jr. (1929–1968), civil rights leader and recipient of the 1964 Nobel Peace Prize. King is a model of integrity; he acted on his convictions and stood up for his beliefs, spreading a message of nonviolence to a nation in turmoil. Most young children won't understand the concept of integrity, but it's important to teach them to do what's right. You can model integrity by talking aloud when making decisions. You might say, "It would be much easier to stay at home and do nothing today, but I really want to donate a few hours to our community center instead."

Today
I'll teach my children what's important.

January 16

**"Sometimes we have to stop dealing with
the misbehavior and heal the relationship first."**
Jane Nelsen, Ed.D.

Young children sometimes kick, shout, scream,
throw tantrums, and act out in other ways to get
attention. Why do they behave like this? Most
young children don't have the words to express
what they're really feeling: angry, frustrated, alone,
unsure. If your child's behavior gets out of hand,
take a deep breath before reacting. Ask yourself
what he or she may be feeling. Is getting mad or
punishing your child truly the answer? Is there
something you could do to help instead?

Today
I'll stay calm.

January 17

**"Books were my pass to personal freedom.
I learned to read at age three and soon discovered
there was a whole world to conquer
that went beyond our farm in Mississippi."**
Oprah Winfrey

Oprah Winfrey loves books and, through her TV
show and magazine, has encouraged others to share
this passion. One of her all-time favorite books is
Toni Morrison's *The Bluest Eye*, a classic that pro-
foundly influenced her understanding of her own
childhood and growing-up years. What books did
you love as a child? How did they affect who you
were then and who you are today? When was the
last time you read those old favorites—or shared
them with a child?

Today

I'll read to a child.

January 18

**"Parents can only give good advice
or put them on the right paths,
but the final forming of a person's character
lies in their own hands."**

Anne Frank

A parent is our first guide in life—the person who helps bring us into the world and teaches us how it works. As adults, we're important guides for young children—our own and those in our care. It's our obligation—and honor—to put children on the right path, and this means, in part, giving them the power to make decisions on their own. Help them to see that they have the power to choose, even if the choice is as simple as, "Do you want a banana or an apple?" Children who feel empowered to make decisions for themselves are off to a great start in life.

Today
I'll give a child the power to choose.

January 19

**"Success has nothing to do
with what you gain in life or accomplish for yourself.
It's what you do for others."**
Danny Thomas

Children feel more connected when their parents are directly involved in their activities. Do you make time to participate in your children's activities at home and away from home? You might take time off from work to help chaperone an outing with your child's preschool, or you might go to a public park or an indoor pool with your child in the evening. On weekends, you could take your child and a few playmates to a local playground. The more you participate, the more your child—and you—will learn.

Today
**I'll do an activity with my child
outside of our home.**

January 20

"I just went ahead doing what I liked to do."
Linus Pauling

Linus Pauling was nine when his father died. His family lived in poverty, so to earn money, he did odd jobs like chopping wood. He doubted he'd ever have the chance for higher education. Despite such adversity, Pauling (winner of the 1954 Nobel Prize in chemistry and the 1962 Nobel Peace Prize) remained enthusiastic and curious. He found his life's passion in science and continued doing what he liked to do. Young children who are tremendously interested in an activity may be on their way to finding *their* passion—one that could last a lifetime. What might you do to affirm this interest?

Today
I'll encourage a child in an activity he or she loves.

COMMITMENT TO LEARNING
ASSET #23: STIMULATING ACTIVITY AND HOMEWORK

January 21

"This is no small task for any adult, even the most caring of us—to begin, even in the first months of life, to teach an infant that others count."
Robert Coles

Infants thrive when their needs are met immediately and consistently. But as they grow, babies come to see that other people count, too. For example, they may have a sibling who also requires feeding, changing, and holding. Sometimes, parents feel guilty when they can't be there for their baby every moment of every day. They may feel as if they're being tugged in too many directions when what they really want to do is focus on their infant. If you feel this way as a parent, remember that your baby is gradually learning that other people have needs—even you. You may find it helpful to get a baby-sitter, so you can spend one-on-one time with your other child or have an hour to yourself.

Today
I'll remember what my baby is learning.

January 22

**"Shortcomings can be changed into good points
if only we set our aims high enough."**
Shinichi Suzuki

Everyone has strengths and weaknesses—even young children. For example, your toddler may have strong fine-motor skills; he or she may find it easy to hold a crayon or pick up small pieces of food. On the other hand, your toddler may have difficulty with large-motor skills like running or climbing the ladder of a slide. It's normal for young children to develop skills at different rates and to be more proficient in some areas than in others. You can help by providing both fine- and large-motor activities that encourage toddlers to hone skills that don't come as easily.

Today
I'll provide fine- and large-motor activities.

January 23

"The only thing of lasting value you can give a child is your time and the memories of the time you shared together."
Jim Trelease

Your young children may ask for toys and candy, but what they really want and need most is your time. They enjoy your attention; they want to inter-act; they love unhurried, unscheduled time with you. The moments you spend together are a gift of lasting value—they'll be remembered long after a toy is broken or a piece of candy is gone. You can say, "Let's have some fun! What do you want to do with me right now?" and let your children choose how to pass the time. Follow their lead and make some memories together.

Today
I'll give my children some focused time.

January 24

"Through music you learn not to care about the color of someone's skin."
Vince Gill

Children can develop prejudices at a young age—long before they're fully aware of them. They notice the attitudes (positive or negative) that the adults who care for them have toward people of different races and cultures. You have the power to help your children grow up with an appreciation of diversity: the people, places, music, art, books, crafts, languages, and traditions you expose children to can make all the difference. Yet, keep in mind that traditional dances, songs, and foods, for example, are only *part* of a culture. Be sure that children understand that members of a cultural group do more than wear special clothing or listen to one kind of music. Together, you can explore other aspects of people's lives as well.

Today
I'll help my children learn about another culture.

SOCIAL COMPETENCIES
ASSET #34: CULTURAL COMPETENCE

January 25

"Neighbors need to discuss how much supervision
or authority they are willing to allow neighbors
to exercise over their children."
Stephanie Mann

In your neighborhood, what happens if preschoolers
who are playing together outside begin to push or
hit? Do the adults in your community feel free to
talk to young children who are acting up? Sometimes, adults turn the other way and say nothing;
they're afraid to step in because they fear offending
other parents. Neighborhood meetings—or simply
meeting your neighbors—will open the lines of
communication. You can get to know each other
and talk about ways to solve problems together.

Today
I'll talk with a neighbor.

January 26

**"It is never too early
to start taking care of yourself."**
Jane Brody

(It's never too late either.) Often, we pay a lot more attention to our children's health than to our own. We watch what they eat, make sure they get exercise, arrange for them to spend time outdoors, and see that they're in bed early. In our efforts to take good care of them, we often forget to take care of *ourselves*. But self-care is essential: you too need a healthy diet, physical activity, outdoor time, and rest. Make it a priority to put yourself first for one hour today—ask a friend to baby-sit so you can. Afterward, you'll feel more alert and refreshed, and better able to give your children your best.

Today
I'll take care of myself.

January 27

**"You have to know your child
and be attentive to the child.
You can help."**
Joseph Campbell

All young children need support, but each child's
specific needs are unique. Some require lots of stimulation and active play; others prefer more quiet
one-on-one moments. Some children love to be held
and cuddled, while others hardly ever sit still on
your lap. To confuse matters, children's needs
change at different ages and stages. Just when you
think you've figured things out, your child needs
something new from you. Raising children isn't
easy, but the rewards are endless!

Today
I'll pay attention to my child's individual needs.

January 28

"It is within the family that children first learn how to get along with people bigger and smaller than they are."
Victoria Secunda

Siblings can get into really BIG fights. Sometimes parents feel like referees in need of very large whistles. While the arguments may drive you crazy, they offer children the chance to learn how to negotiate and get along better with older or younger kids. You can say, "I know you both want to play with that, but let's take turns." Or "Hitting doesn't solve problems. Let's think of another way to work this out." Teaching children to resolve conflicts peacefully at home gives them skills they can use at school, in the community, and throughout their lives.

Today
I'll see an argument as an opportunity.

SOCIAL COMPETENCIES
ASSET #36: PEACEFUL CONFLICT RESOLUTION

January 29

"The only way to have a friend is to be one."
Ralph Waldo Emerson

As toddlers, children begin interacting with other children their age. Although they may not communicate well at this age or understand the importance of sharing toys, toddlers learn what it means to have a friend. Preschoolers are able to learn basic friendship skills, and they enjoy being social. Compliment children when they play together well. You can show them that friends care and share. And you can teach them that the best way to have a friend is to *be* a friend.

Today
I'll help children be friendly.

January 30

"Learning is wealth that can't be stolen."
Philippine proverb

Learning something is valuable. Enjoying the process of learning is *in*valuable. When young children see that you're fascinated by facts, knowledge, or new information, they witness the power of learning, and they'll want to experience this themselves. Encourage their curiosity and questions. If you don't know an answer, let children see that you'll dig to help them find it. Go to the library together, explore a child-friendly Web site, or consult an expert. No one is ever too old or too young to learn.

Today
I'll answer a child's questions.

January 31

**"You are your most valuable asset.
Don't forget that. You are the best thing you have."**
Gary Paulsen

What's the most important role you'll ever play? Being a parent? A caregiver? A teacher? Nope: being *yourself.* This is the most important role anyone plays in life, and it's true for children, too. Be sure that you continue to develop your own interests, skills, and goals—this keeps you connected to who you are. Encourage your children to be who *they* are and to recognize what makes them unique. Let them know you love and value them just for being themselves.

Today
I'll value children's unique qualities.

February 1

**"Encouragement is teaching children the life skills
they need to be successful in life and relationships."**
Jane Nelsen, Ed.D.

February 1 is Be an Encourager Day. Mark your
calendar or put "Be encouraging" on today's to-do
list as a reminder. Encouragement can mean a
phone call to a sick friend or a thank you to someone you depend on at work; it can mean a compliment or a pat on the back—you can even make
encouragement a daily habit. Be sure to encourage a
child, especially one who least expects it. You might
say, "Go ahead and try it. I know you can do it!" Or
"Look at that. You put the puzzle together all by
yourself!" And by modeling encouragement, you're
more likely to raise a child who will encourage
others—even you!

Today
I'll be encouraging.

SOCIAL COMPETENCIES
ASSET #33: INTERPERSONAL SKILLS

February 2

*"You have to take your little piece of the world
that needs to be worked on
and do the best you can, whatever it is."*
Janet McCloud

Louise Helton noticed that children in her daughter's first-grade class were lagging behind in their learning. When she discovered that her state of Nevada ranked last in preschool funding and didn't require children to attend kindergarten, she took action. She bought a bus and created a mobile preschool to reach kids in different neighborhoods. Thanks to corporate funding, Louise Helton now has six preschool buses in her fleet—serving more than 400 children from twenty-three neighborhoods throughout the Las Vegas area. She proved that anyone can take action—everyone can serve. What might you do?

Today

I'll do my part to serve children.

February 3

**"The ability to concentrate
and to use your time well is everything."**
Lee Iacocca

When children have their basic needs met, they concentrate better. They're more able to get caught up in learning and active play. You can make sure that the children in your care are well rested and are eating nutrient-rich foods. You can notice if certain stressors are affecting their ability to focus. Children's basic needs come first; learning then follows.

Today
I'll pay attention to children's basic needs.

COMMITMENT TO LEARNING
ASSET #22: CHILDREN ARE ENGAGED IN LEARNING

February 4

"Good programs build skills in a child while also educating parents about what their infant can do."
Roni Leiderman, Ph.D.

You may have an infant who's involved in a child-care program or who spends time with a caregiver each day. Do you know what your child does during this time away from home? Some childcare centers provide regular written notes about what babies have been up to during the day; others rely on conversations with parents when they arrive to pick up their children. If your center or caregiver doesn't already use a written or verbal system for keeping parents up to date, you might suggest implementing one. You can also make a point of spending a few moments talking about your baby and asking questions when you pick him or her up.

Today
I'll ask a caregiver about my child's day.

February 5

> "The more secure and accepted [a child] feels among friends, the easier it will be for him to disagree with them."
> *Stanley I. Greenspan, M.D.*

Between the ages of three and five, children begin to learn social rules and gain a better understanding of what is and isn't acceptable. But even young children can be influenced by peer pressure. Following a friend's lead, your preschooler may bully, grab toys, or color on the walls, even if he or she has been told that these actions are inappropriate. In response, you might say, "It's okay to say no to a friend. You can do what *you* know is right." As children play together, they learn together, and sometimes this means figuring out how to set boundaries.

Today
I'll be mindful of peer pressure.

SOCIAL COMPETENCIES
ASSET #35: RESISTANCE SKILLS

February 6

"Follow your bliss."
Joseph Campbell

Do you tend to put off those activities that make you feel awake and alive? Do you tell yourself you can't dance because the dishes aren't done, can't paint until you've polished the furniture? Do you say no to a game with your child, because there's paperwork to finish or laundry to do? If you've got a household to run and work to be done, you may feel that it isn't possible to make time for fun activities. But did you know that time spent on something that gives you pleasure actually renews your energy and sense of purpose? So follow your bliss! And invite your children to do the same.

Today
I'll take time for pleasure.

February 7

**"It's important for the kids to have role models
who go to the same supermarket
and live on the same block."**
Geoffrey Canada

Geoffrey Canada cares about children in the New York City neighborhood where he grew up. After finishing his education, he returned to his old neighborhood, with its familiar poverty and problems. Determined to help, he now works in social services on behalf of children. He also teaches a martial-arts class twice a week to help children gain self-confidence and self-defense skills. Geoffrey Canada isn't a sports hero or a celebrity, but plenty of kids look up to him: he's the role model right next door. You can be, too.

Today
I'll be a role model to children in my neighborhood.

February 8

**"We are often misguided by the inappropriate goal
of seeking to control students rather than
empowering them to control themselves."**
Charlotte Reed and David Strahan

Children's lives are filled with rules: *Don't grab.
Don't talk with your mouth full. Don't hog all the blocks.*
They hear a lot of "don'ts" but may not understand
the "whys" behind them. If you need children to
quiet down, you can say it positively and explain
why it's important. Children who hear, "Let's use
our indoor voices, so we don't disturb other people
in the library" are more likely to respect boundaries
than those who are told, "Hush up!" In your classroom, childcare center, or home, make it the rule to
set positive rules. Use "do's" instead of "don'ts," so
children feel empowered.

Today
I'll set boundaries in a positive way.

February 9

"When one helps another, both gain strength."
Ecuadorian proverb

One of Mary Guthrie's sons was born with a seizure disorder and developmental problems. Another was hearing impaired. When they were grown, she created Giant Step, a childcare center for children with special needs—a place like the one she wished she could have taken her own sons to. Mary Guthrie paved the way for children who are often overlooked. What other paths do we need to forge on behalf of children? Which inequalities do we need to address? How can we promote equality for all children?

Today
I'll identify a children's equality issue— and think about how I can help.

February 10

**"Children grow well
when their parents are growing well."**
W. D. Wall

Our young children rely on us to meet all of their physical and emotional needs; they look to us for support. What if stressors in our own lives—difficulties at work, care of an aging parent, money problems, health issues—leave us preoccupied and unable to move forward? Children pick up on this stress; it affects their well-being. If you need help coping with stressors in your life, you can ask for it. Turn to a friend, relative, counselor, or religious advisor. When you get help for yourself, you help your children, too.

Today
I'll get help if I need it.

February 11

"A negative attitude is a true handicap."
Crenner Bradley

The world is made up of optimists and pessimists, and you probably know plenty of both. Experts say that a positive outlook can lead to a happier, healthier life. Show children how mistakes can be learning experiences, how problems can be opportunities. You might say, "Oops, your shoes are on the wrong feet. Can I show you a trick to help you learn which way they go?" Or "Everyone spills juice once in a while. Let's work together to clean it up." Encourage young children to look on the bright side, even (or especially) if they tend to take a pessimistic view.

Today
I'll model a positive attitude.

POSITIVE IDENTITY
ASSET #40: POSITIVE VIEW OF PERSONAL FUTURE

February 12

"If I were two-faced, would I be wearing this one?"
Abraham Lincoln

Before he was elected president, Abraham Lincoln and a partner bought a store on credit. The store failed and put the men deep into debt. When his partner died, Lincoln took on *his* debt, too, and worked for years until he had paid off all that both men owed. His high standard of truthfulness earned Lincoln—born on this day—the nickname "Honest Abe." Honesty doesn't come easy, especially to young children. They often see nothing wrong with telling a lie to get the result they want or to avoid punishment. If your child lies, you might say, "When I hear something that isn't true, I feel concerned. Let's talk about what *really* happened."

Today
I'll help my child tell the truth.

February 13

"We must rearrange our mode of living
so that children become true and considered
members of the community."
Margaret Mead

Young children in many communities are silent
residents. They — and the people who care for
them — may have worthwhile opinions and ideas,
but often go unheard. Communities that are inten-
tional about bringing out the best in young children
understand this. Some communities even have
focus groups to ask preschoolers what they would
like to see in a new playground or park; other
communities make a point of gathering the
opinions of parents, childcare workers, and teachers
and inviting them to help make decisions. This
ensures that *everyone* in the community has a voice.
How can your community engage young children?

Today
I'll ask for a child's, parent's, or caregiver's opinion.

EMPOWERMENT
ASSET #7: COMMUNITY VALUES CHILDREN

February 14

"Whether our children become solid, loving, and responsible grownups depends, in the end, on how well we love them as they grow."
Colin Greer

Young children love Valentine's Day and the giving and receiving of cards that say "I love you" or "You're special." Months after this holiday, children may still look at old valentines to be reminded of who loves and supports them. They may repeatedly ask, "Who gave me this one?" or "What does this one say?" Valentine's Day is a great excuse for lots of hugs, kisses, cuddles, and loving cards. Make the most of this day!

Today
I'll make valentines with and for my children.

February 15

"Imagine what a harmonious world it could be if every single person, both young and old, shared a little of what he is good at doing."

Quincy Jones

The statement "Take responsibility" can sound foreboding. We may equate taking responsibility with doing some task we dread. But what if each one of us took responsibility for doing something we're *good at*—something we *enjoy?* What if we found fun ways to share our skills (woodworking, crafts, piano, storytelling) with young children to help them learn and grow? Go ahead and "Take responsibility"!

Today
I'll share a skill of mine with children.

February 16

> **"[A] child's progress was known
> to the whole clan . . . and the child grew
> to adulthood with a sense of reputation
> to sustain."**
>
> *Ohiyesa*

Ohiyesa, a Santee Sioux who was instrumental in founding the Boy Scouts of America and the Campfire Girls, spoke of how children of the Sioux tradition were always kept in the public eye. Parents announced the birth of their child to the community and made similar announcements for the child's first step, first word, and other developments. You can follow traditions like these in your neighborhood or community by sharing children's milestones. Publish birth announcements in your local paper; let your toddler show off his first trike ride; hang balloons on your mailbox to honor your child's birthday, and then invite the neighbors for cake and ice cream.

Today
I'll share the news of my child's "firsts."

February 17

"I love myself when I am laughing."
Zora Neale Hurston

February is National Boost Your Self-Esteem Month. If you've got the winter blues or feel cooped up indoors, find ways to raise your spirits. Bundle up your children and take them outside to play, even if it's cold and wet or slushy and snowy. Laugh together as you make snowpeople or simply take a short walk. The fresh air will revive you, and the outdoor time will help your children release energy. Afterward, go indoors and read funny stories aloud. You'll all feel much better.

Today
I'll think of an activity to boost our spirits.

February 18

**"A loving, caring teacher took a liking to me.
She noticed the potential [in me]
and wanted to help shape it."**
Tom Bradley

Caring adults—childcare providers, preschool teachers, librarians—are the key to creating positive environments for children. Maybe you're a caregiver yourself, or maybe you're a parent (or both). If you're a parent, remember to ask your child's caregivers how they're doing and to thank them for a job well done. If you're a caregiver, take time to get to know the children's parents through conferences and conversations. Supporting each other in these ways helps you better support your kids.

Today
I'll support a caregiver or parent.

February 19

"Live to learn and you will learn to live."
Portuguese proverb

The Carnegie Task Force on Meeting the Needs of
Young Children states that many young children
don't get enough stimulation. For example, only 50
percent of infants and toddlers are read to on a
regular basis. The same task force concluded that,
because of a lack of stimulation, 35 percent of
children start their first day of kindergarten unpre-
pared to learn. What to do? Read to children, make
play dough with them, show them how to use
safety scissors, give them blocks to build with and
pages to color. Do whatever you can to get them
thinking and learning.

Today
I'll stimulate a child.

February 20

> **"You're teaching your children about sexuality every day, even if you don't realize it."**
> *Jamie Wasserman*

Developing a healthy sense of sexuality begins at home. Long before children are able to understand the facts of life, they're learning about how adults express affection. When we hug and hold our children, they learn that physical touch is a way to show caring. They see how we, as parents, hug, kiss, or caress each other; how we use our eyes and words to convey love and respect. Remember that children are watching—and learning from—these expressions.

Today
I'll be aware of my body language.

February 21

"La gente hablando se entiende."
"People understand one another by talking."
Southwestern Spanish proverb

People also understand each other by *listening*. An air of openness and trust leads to better communication in families, childcare centers, preschools, neighborhoods, and communities. When we value what young children have to say—including the cries of an infant or the "nos" of a toddler—we create an open and trusting environment. In your home, ensure that your children have a voice and feel comfortable expressing themselves. Talk and listen.

Today
I'll focus on good communication.

February 22

"Fear is an inborn reaction to a possible danger."
James M. Herzog, M.D.

Young children have a lot of fears. Infants startle when they hear loud noises; toddlers shy away from strangers; preschoolers may be scared of the dark. It's easy to dismiss such fears if you know the loud noise was a truck, that the stranger is actually a friend, or that darkness doesn't mean danger. Dismissing what frightens children doesn't help them feel safer—taking the fears seriously does. For example, help your child overcome a fear of the dark by exploring the room before bedtime and pointing out that there's nothing frightening in the closet or under the bed. You can leave a night-light on and give your child a Teddy bear or other soft toy to hold close during the night.

Today
I'll soothe my child's fears.

February 23

**"Nothing is going to be handed to you.
You have to make things happen."**
Florence Griffith Joyner

Everyone fantasizes about sudden success. Who hasn't dreamed of winning the lottery or having their wishes come true? But success almost always takes planning and hard work. Olympic medalists don't accomplish great feats because they ran around the track once or twice, or dove into a pool occasionally. They practiced—long and hard. Children who learn the value of "sticking to it" have a better chance of success in life. Encourage young children to keep trying, even if their task seems difficult. Say, "Sometimes it's hard to put all of the game pieces away. I know you can do it if you keep trying."

Today
I'll remind a child to "stick to it."

COMMITMENT TO LEARNING
ASSET #21: ACHIEVEMENT EXPECTATION AND MOTIVATION

February 24

"Nonviolence is a plant of slow growth."
Mahatma Gandhi

Teaching young children to resolve conflicts peacefully takes years. Children may hit, kick, or bite—even after you just asked them to stop. You can teach children that trying to control someone else by force isn't the way. Children need to focus on what they *can* control: themselves. You can tell them that kicking, hitting, biting, and pushing create more problems; you can show them that taking deep breaths or breaks from one another can help release angry feelings safely. Teach these concepts to children again and again, and over time, they'll learn.

Today
I'll teach a child a way to release anger safely.

February 25

"Parents need to think through what they want
from their religious commitment.
It helps to know as clearly as possible
what you hope your child will gain
from the experience."
Michael Schulman, Ph.D.

What do you want your children to gain from being part of a religious community? Do you want them to interact with people of different generations? To learn about positive values? To grow spiritually? All of the above? Congregations often help people articulate what they believe in and value. When you know what you want from your religious commitment, you're more able to help your children understand its importance in their lives and in yours.

Today
I'll consider what my religious commitment
means to my family.

February 26

"Ain't nothin' to it but to do it."
Maya Angelou

Researcher Suzanne Ziegler found that parents who participate in their children's school activities and provide encouragement for learning at home have a greater impact on their children's achievement. In fact, parent involvement can play a bigger role in achievement than children's ability or their family's socioeconomic status. Show your children—and their teachers and caregivers—that you think learning is important. Get involved by volunteering at their preschool or childcare center, participating in field trips, pointing out helpful resources, or being a resource yourself. Just do it!

Today
I'll support my children's learning.

February 27

"Kids know, better than grownups, what we do is more important than what we say."
Pete Seeger

Young children are like sponges, soaking up everything adults say and do. You may be surprised if your toddler constantly asks for junk food; you may worry if your preschooler seems to watch too much television. At times like these, ask yourself if your actions sometimes speak louder than your words. For example, do you turn on the TV when you need to relax? Do you often snack on chips or cookies in front of your children? Your children may be more tuned in to your words, moods, and actions than you realize.

Today
I'll pay close attention to what I do and say.

POSITIVE VALUES
ASSET #28: FAMILY VALUES INTEGRITY

February 28

> "We have talked at each other
> and about each other for a long time.
> It's high time we all began talking with each other."
> *Bill Clinton*

People who share the same race, religion, or culture tend to spend time together. While this is helpful in creating a strong identity, it may make it more difficult to come together with people of other heritages. In the U.S., February is Black History Month, a time to celebrate achievements and reflect on the past. Spend time reading books about famous black Americans; engage children in activities that create awareness. Give children dolls of different ethnicities to play with; attend a Black History Month event for children. It's time to build bridges instead of walls.

Today
I'll commemorate Black History Month.

February 29

"When there's no one around to enforce the rules,
kids may find it interesting to see
just what happens when they bypass them."
Caroline Chinlund, Ph.D.

You've probably heard about the "terrible twos" and
the "frustrating fours." As children grow, they go
through periods when they're more defiant, more
apt to challenge rules, more persistent about saying
no. During these times, you may become so tired of
disciplining that you're tempted to let things slide.
But consistency is crucial because children won't
respect boundaries they can break. When you're
consistent, you treat the same behavior in the same
way—no matter where you are or what time of day.
Don't give up.

Today
I'll be firm about boundaries.

BOUNDARIES AND EXPECTATIONS
ASSET #11: FAMILY BOUNDARIES

March 1

**"Getting away and calling for help
are children's primary defenses."**
Stephanie Mann

As adults, we know the importance of constantly supervising the young children in our care. But as children reach preschool age, they need to learn two important skills: asking for help and running away from danger. You might ask them a "what if" question: "What if you got lost in the grocery store?" Talk about the options: "You could ask a nearby adult for help," or "You could shout for your mom or dad." Another question might be: "What if a stranger told you to get in his car?" Talk honestly about stranger danger and the importance of shouting for help or running away when frightened. Repeat these questions and messages often to reinforce them.

Today
I'll teach preschoolers one way to resist danger.

March 2

"Oh, the places you'll go!"
Dr. Seuss

March 2 is the birth anniversary of Theodor Seuss Geisel, known to the world as Dr. Seuss. His well-loved books have sold more than 200 million copies and have been translated into twenty languages. Many childcare centers and preschools celebrate March 2 as Dr. Seuss Day—a day to enjoy the wonderful pictures, stories, and rhymes he created. His books take people young and old to places where the imagination can soar and reading is pure fun. Spend time reading Dr. Seuss books with children—you'll all enjoy the ride!

Today
I'll read and imagine with children.

March 3

"Through grandparents, children also learn
how their society keeps going, and what keeps it
strong and steady generation after generation."
Margaret Mead

A young child who has a grandparent is lucky—this
kind of relationship is special for each of them.
Grandparents can provide what parents sometimes
can't: undivided attention. If you're busy or overwhelmed, ask your child's grandparent to visit and
help out—a grandparent can be a wonderful source
of support for both you and your child. If his or her
grandparent lives far away or is unable to help with
a young child who has lots of energy, find ways to
encourage their relationship: arrange for quiet
visits, send photos, write letters describing what
your child is doing, or have your child draw a
picture. Time devoted to a grandparent helps your
child get to know another caring adult and learn
more about the family.

Today
I'll reach out to my child's grandparent.

March 4

**"In meeting a child's emotional needs,
we give him or her the emotional freedom
to meet the needs of others."**
Alfie Kohn

Although caring can be taught, caring first must be "caught." In other words, we don't become caring people unless we've experienced caring ourselves. Infants experience caring when they're held or when they cry and their needs are met. Young children experience caring when they sit on an adult's lap to hear stories and songs. Our caring actions help set the stage for children's emotional growth. Caring is a gift—one that everyone deserves.

Today
I'll show caring.

March 5

"Really great people make you feel that you, too, can become great."
Mark Twain

Children look for role models whose words and actions they admire. As preschoolers, children may talk about sports stars, singers, or even cartoon heroes, but they *most* admire adults they know personally—parents, relatives, teachers, caregivers, religious leaders, or family friends. Are you a role model for the children in your life? You can make sure your words and actions are worth emulating. You can show children that you value being kind and helping others feel good. Children want to look up to you—and they will.

Today
I'll be a role model.

March 6

"We must not . . . ignore the small daily differences
we can make which, over time, add up to big
differences that we often cannot foresee."
Marian Wright Edelman

Power isn't only for people with titles or money.
Anyone can have *personal* power. Personal power is
about making good choices, taking responsibility
for your actions, and standing up for yourself—
little by little, day by day. It's about believing in
your ability to make a difference—even a small
one—in your own life and in the lives of others. To
teach personal power to young children, point out
instances when their actions have positive effects:
"Thank you for picking up your toys like that! The
room looks much nicer, and now we won't trip on
any toys." This helps young children believe, "I can
use my power to be helpful."

Today
I'll help a child feel empowered.

POSITIVE IDENTITY
ASSET #37: PERSONAL POWER

March 7

"Leisure is essential to everyone."
Matt Gold

What if you were granted twenty minutes right now to do something relaxing? Would you take a nap, go for a bike ride, read, talk with a friend? How would your child relax for twenty minutes? Probably by continuing to play and explore. How might you unwind *together?* Snuggle up with a book, play chase, take a leisurely walk, hang out in the park or yard? Why not take twenty minutes (or more) to relax with each other today? You both deserve it.

Today
I'll relax with my child.

March 8

**"I am motivated and inspired
by young people and children.
My eyes light up whenever children come around."**
Rosa Parks

March is Youth Art Month, a time to recognize how fun and empowering art can be. Help older babies scribble with crayons. Encourage toddlers and preschoolers to finger paint, color, draw, or make simple collages using colorful tissue paper and glue. So much of what young children do is a work of art. Let your eyes light up as they show you their pictures; admire the effort and the end result. You can showcase their talents by displaying their artwork on the wall or refrigerator. Let them see how their beautiful work livens up your home, school, or childcare center.

Today
I'll help children create and display art.

EMPOWERMENT
ASSET #8: CHILDREN ARE GIVEN USEFUL ROLES

March 9

"At the playground, Wemberly worried about the chains on the swings, and the bolts on the slide, and the bars on the jungle gym."
Kevin Henkes

In the picture book *Wemberly Worried,* young Wemberly mouse worries about nearly everything. Worries are normal for young children. They may feel anxious about anything from animals to water, and they need the help and reassurance of an adult to face what bothers them. A child who's anxious about animals can spend a small amount of supervised time with other people's dogs or cats, or visit a petting zoo with you. At a public pool, a child can dip his or her toes in the water to get used to it, and then be held close as you gradually explore the shallow end together. Your gentle encouragement will help a young child gain confidence while learning more about the world.

Today

I'll help a child learn to cope with a worry.

March 10

**"It is important for teachers not to simply issue
the rules, but to teach and model the rules."**
Edward Wynne and Kevin Ryan

Many classrooms and childcare centers have rules
about using indoor voices or walking in the halls.
But what happens when teachers or caregivers raise
their voices to communicate across the room or to
get a child's attention? What happens if they run
down the hallway to answer the phone? This sends
a mixed message to young children who learn by
what we say *and* what we do. You might say,
"Whoops! I'm talking too loud. I have to remember
to use my indoor voice, don't I?" Or "I ran down
the hall because I was in a hurry, but I could have
tripped and hurt myself." Let children see that rules
apply to you just like everyone else.

Today
I'll model the rules.

March 11

**"The last of the human freedoms: to choose
one's attitude in any given set of circumstances,
to choose one's own way."**
Viktor Frankl

For three years during World War II, Viktor Frankl
lived at Auschwitz and other Nazi prison camps.
Separated from his family, he saw many people
suffer and die. After he was released, he learned
that his entire family had been killed. Viktor Frankl
could have been bitter, but instead he drew from his
experience to become a leading thinker in medical
and psychiatric circles. His best-selling book,
Man's Search for Meaning, explores the importance
of finding a sense of purpose. Let your children see
that you, too, are positive and enthusiastic about
life—that you believe your life, and theirs, has
meaning.

Today
I'll continue to search for my sense of purpose.

March 12

"Everyone needs help from everyone."
Bertolt Brecht

By nature, young children are self-centered. Focusing on their own wants and needs helps them to form a strong sense of self. But as children grow, they're more able to develop their sense of caring and service to others. Preschoolers like to help with small chores at home, when given the chance; they take pride in teaching a playmate a skill they've already mastered. Helping others builds young children's self-esteem. Empower them to be of service to others by showing them specific ways to help. Be sure to notice and say something positive when children lend a hand.

Today
I'll encourage a child to be helpful.

EMPOWERMENT
ASSET #9: SERVICE TO OTHERS

March 13

"Where is there dignity unless there is honesty?"
Cicero

We admire people who act with dignity and honesty. We respect their consistency, their ability to own up to their mistakes. Young children can learn the value of honesty early on. While reading books or watching TV together, point out the behavior of the characters. Ask children, "Is this person honest?" "Does she tell the truth or tell lies?" "How does he treat other people?" "Would you want to be like that person?" "Why or why not?" Help your children see that your family values honesty.

Today
I'll reinforce the importance of being truthful.

March 14

"Say yes to mess."
Stanley I. Greenspan, M.D.

Between the ages of three and five, children become more coordinated and their fine-motor skills increase. They enjoy working with their hands, and they have better control of them, too. March is National Craft Month, so use this time to try a new craft or resurrect an old favorite—and make a mess! Have fun as you and your children work with paint, chalk, glitter, glue, wood, or fabric. You can even designate a room or table just for arts and crafts, so setup and cleanup are a snap.

Today
I'll be "crafty."

March 15

"Won't you be my neighbor?"
Fred Rogers

At the beginning of the TV program *Mister Rogers' Neighborhood,* Fred Rogers invites young viewers in as he hangs up his jacket, slips on a comfortable sweater, and changes his dress shoes to sneakers. All the while, he sings a song that asks, "Won't you be my neighbor?" Through this carefully crafted entrance, he helps young children understand that it's important to be neighborly and to welcome others. Show children that this message is important in your home, too. Invite your child's playmates over often, or bake cookies or other treats with your child and bring them over to a neighbor's home to share.

Today
I'll be neighborly.

March 16

**"Once the 'what' is decided,
the 'how' always follows."**
Pearl S. Buck

When children make a decision, we often think
they're done with the choosing. Yet, a whole new
range of decisions opens up once the first one
occurs. For example, a preschooler may pick a red
marker, and then proceed to color his or her hands.
While you may not like this decision, you can relax
and see the imagination that the child is tapping
into. You might react by gently saying, "That's a
beautiful color you chose, but it will last longer on
your paper than on your hands." Good decision-
making skills take lots of time to learn. Be patient.

Today
**I'll be open to the creative decisions
that children make.**

SOCIAL COMPETENCIES
ASSET #32: PLANNING AND DECISION MAKING

March 17

> "Exhibits can help develop learning skills. . . .
> They're a fun way for families
> to spend time together."
>
> *Rochel Gelman*

At the Habitot Children's Museum in Berkeley, California, young visitors get hands-on experience with wind tunnels and water-pumping stations. Infants and toddlers at the Boston Children's Museum can participate in weekly music and movement programs. Children put on raincoats at Chicago's Children's Museum to build a dam, spray water, and generally get wet. Throughout North America, children's museums offer safe creative activities, a chance for discovery, and social time with other kids. And the museums aren't just for children—adults can have plenty of fun, too! Why not explore an exhibit together?

Today
I'll make plans to visit a children's exhibit.

March 18

**"To have a good friend
is one of the highest delights of life."**
Anonymous

How do you feel when you're with people you care about, who you can talk with at length, who like you for who you are? Most likely, you feel comfortable, inspired, and joyful. Good friends enrich your life; they help you feel at home in the world. Young children are enriched when they see you modeling friendship—and when they have good friends of their own. Preschoolers especially need friends, because at this age, children become more social. Help children find playmates: they'll enjoy having friends their own age to laugh, explore, and play make-believe with.

Today
I'll arrange a play date for my child.

March 19

"All children are musicians;
all children are artists."
Susan Castro

Children love to make music. One of the joys of
being around young children is hearing them sing
and watching them dance. Musical activities
encourage young children to be spontaneous and
daring—and let *you* explore your own creative side.
Take time to sing or play instruments with your
children; share with them the fun of playing soft
and loud, low and high; introduce them to favorite
children's musicians such as Raffi and Ella Jenkins.
(P.S. March is Music in Our Schools Month.)

Today
I'll make music.

March 20

**"My friends, how desperately do we need
to be loved and to love."**
Chief Dan George

Do you sometimes take love for granted? Some
days, do you forget to say "I love you" or to give
hugs and kisses? Young children (and older ones,
too) need to hear the words and feel your touch. In
fact, for infants and young children, touch is more
powerful than any words. You can demonstrate
love in many ways: by holding your baby close,
letting your toddler climb up on your lap, and
kissing your preschooler good-night before bed.
Show affection as often as you can and let your
children feel how much you care.

Today
I'll be loving.

March 21

**"There are 25 million Americans that are hungry,
who go to food banks and soup kitchens,
and half of them are under the age of seventeen."**
Tony Hall

Every community has people who are homeless
and hungry—many of whom are children. Can you
help? Local shelters and food shelves are always in
need of volunteers. What about bringing your
preschooler along while you give of your time?
Although you may feel that a child should be
protected from the harsh realities of hunger and
homelessness, volunteering this way can be a
wonderful lesson about the power of community
service. You can show children that people of *all*
ages can do their part.

Today
I'll consider volunteering with my child.

March 22

"For children under the age of five, constant adult supervision ensures safety."
Nancy Leffert, Ph.D.

Many neighborhoods have clubs or groups that help parents of young children get to know other families. These groups often meet in members' homes or at a nearby community center; the adults share anecdotes and information, while the children play nearby. If you'd like to join this type of group, see if your neighborhood association, community center, or YMCA/YWCA has some information. Connecting with moms and dads who live nearby is important, but so is keeping an eye on the children while you meet. Be sure that they have plenty of supervision—you may even want to hire someone to help watch and entertain the children while the adults chat.

Today

I'll make sure children are supervised when adults meet.

BOUNDARIES AND EXPECTATIONS
ASSET #13: NEIGHBORHOOD BOUNDARIES

March 23

**"That is what our children can offer us,
and what we can offer them:
a chance to learn from them,
even as we try to teach them."**
Robert Coles

Even young children can teach adults. Infants show us the importance of living in the moment; toddlers share with us the excitement of stepping in puddles or finding worms on rainy days; preschoolers teach us to stop working so hard and play a game of Hide and Seek. And *all* children remind us of the importance of patience and understanding. Learning is a give-and-take process. Teaching involves not only leading the way but also following the interesting paths children lead us to.

Today
I'll be open to what a young child can teach me.

March 24

"Because they are children and for no other reason they have dignity and worth simply because they are."
Barbara Coloroso

How do young children contribute to community life? Watch what happens when an infant is brought into a roomful of people. Many in the room will automatically smile and head toward the baby; some may even ask to hold him or her. Infants, just by showing up, can bring out warmth in people. The same is true when toddlers and preschoolers enter a room. The people who are gathered may smile, say hello, or ask, "How are you today?" These friendly greetings help young children feel like welcome members of the community.

Today
I'll greet children warmly.

March 25

"There is no resource more precious to this country than our children, and no factor more important to our children's health than good nutrition."
Michael F. Jacobson

Good nutrition not only helps children to grow up healthy and strong but also helps prevent disease later on. You can give young children a good start in life by making sure they eat a variety of fruits and vegetables, in addition to other nutritious foods, every day. Put limits on the number of sugary treats and high-sodium foods that your children consume. Exercise is also an important part of a healthy lifestyle, so make sure your children have lots of playtime—outdoors whenever possible.

Today
I'll put nutrition first.

March 26

"A positive school climate encourages communication, creativity, achievement, and acceptance of others."
Sue Keister

Programs for young children often don't get as much attention in communities as the elementary, middle-school, and high-school ones do. Yet these programs have a big impact on the toddlers and preschoolers they serve. Have you looked into the educational opportunities in your area (community-education programs, preschools, Montessori schools)? If you have a young child, get him or her involved in a caring educational program. If you don't have a child, offer to read books to children at a preschool or another program several times a year. Your involvement can make these places even warmer and friendlier for young children.

Today

I'll see what educational opportunities my community offers.

March 27

"In caring for others,
we nourish our own self-esteem."
Jessamyn West

Building relationships is essential for building self-esteem—when you connect with others, you feel better about yourself. And when you connect with children in particular, you feel younger and more lively. Enjoy the time you spend with children; remember what a precious opportunity it is to teach them, play with them, and read to them. You'll feel a warm sense of satisfaction when a child smiles at you, gives you a hug, or takes you by the hand.

Today

I'll notice how I feel when I care for a child.

March 28

**"I'm not an American hero.
I'm a person that loves children."**
Mother Hale

Some role models never make the headlines and are hardly ever hailed as heroes. Who are they? Childcare providers, preschool teachers, foster parents, and volunteers who read to young children at the library or help monitor the neighborhood bus stops each morning—people who care for and love children day by day. Be sure to recognize these important individuals and give them the thanks they deserve. (And if you're one of these people yourself, kudos to you.)

Today
**I'll thank someone who's making
a difference to children.**

BOUNDARIES AND EXPECTATIONS
ASSET #14: ADULT ROLE MODELS

March 29

**"People can say what they like
about the eternal verities, love and truth and so on,
but nothing's as eternal as the dishes."**
Margaret Mahy

Young children learn by watching how parents and caregivers prepare meals, clean up, and take care of the center or home. Maybe you push yourself too hard to get things done, or maybe you do less than your best. A toddler or preschooler will notice how you handle your tasks, so remember that you're setting an example. Invite children to help you with chores: toddlers can learn to put away toys, and preschoolers can wipe the table or feed a pet. This teaches responsibility and helps young children learn to be helpful.

Today
**I'll pay attention to what I'm teaching
about daily chores.**

March 30

"When we really listen to our children without constantly judging or correcting them, we let our kids know that we value them."
Margaret Mackenzie, Ph.D.

When young children begin to learn how to talk, it's important to stop, look, and listen—even if we don't completely understand what they're saying. Young children often communicate through gestures, facial expressions, and body movements as they grasp for words; it's important to be attuned to what they're trying to express. By working to understand what young children are communicating—instead of trying to correct their language—we learn what they need and feel. March is International Listening Awareness Month, so let's give children our full attention.

Today
I'll look and listen as children express themselves.

March 31

**"Intellect cannot work at its best
without emotional intelligence."**
Daniel Goleman

For years, many people emphasized the importance
of being "smart"; they thought that if you got a
good education, you'd go far in life. Then, in 1995,
Daniel Goleman published the book *Emotional
Intelligence,* which revolutionized the way we look
at intelligence and emotions. Emotional intelligence
is about being empathetic and self-aware, handling
feelings and stress, communicating well, and
resolving conflicts fairly—skills that take years for
people to learn. You can help young children get a
good start with these skills by showing them how to
recognize emotions and give them a name: "I'm
mad." "I'm sad." "I'm glad." Model how to express
these feelings in healthy ways.

Today
I'll help a child name his or her emotions.

April 1

"All children need time in which they're not expected to perform, produce, behave, or learn."
Kyle Pruett

Humor is a great way to connect with young children. Babies will giggle if you make funny faces or play Peekaboo. Toddlers will laugh with delight if you say, "Here kitty, kitty" to the dog. Preschoolers will get a kick out of watching you do silly dances to their favorite songs. When you make your children smile and laugh, you'll start smiling and laughing, too, and all of you will feel good. April Fool's Day is the perfect excuse to lighten up and loosen up.

Today
I'll laugh with my children.

April 2

*"Children need not only food, clothing, and shelter
but also purpose and principles to hold high
and give direction and meaning to life."*
Robert Coles

The U.S. Department of Agriculture estimates that
it costs $242,890 for a family to raise a child from
birth to the age of eighteen. The expense may seem
overwhelming, causing some parents to doubt
whether they can ever give their children enough
in life. Yet, there are things any parent can give a
child, regardless of the family's financial situation:
positive values, love, limits, and stimulating activities. These things don't cost money, and they have
a huge payback. Children who grow up with these
benefits feel supported and valued—the most precious gifts of all.

Today
I'll know what's truly important to give.

April 3

**"Children come into the world not knowing
who they are. They learn who they are
from those around them."**
Katherine Kersey

When activist and educator Parker J. Palmer's
granddaughter was born a few years ago, he began
jotting observations about her personality, interests,
and likes and dislikes. Palmer plans to write his
granddaughter a letter about all of these observations when she reaches her late teens or early twenties. He hopes his words will help her remember
who she was when she was younger and "reclaim
the gift of true self." Consider writing a letter to a
young child you know, describing some fun observations you've made or the hopes you have for his
or her future. You can deliver the letter in person
and read it out loud as the child sits on your lap.

Today
I'll write to a child.

BOUNDARIES AND EXPECTATIONS
ASSET #14: ADULT ROLE MODELS

April 4

**"Remember that everyone's life is measured
by the power that that individual has
to make the world better."**
Booker T. Washington

Young children can learn about their power to make
a positive difference. While taking a walk or playing
at the park with children, point out the litter you see
(soda cans, snack bags). You might say, "Let's pick
that up and put it in the garbage where it belongs."
Back at home or in the classroom, notice children's
positive interactions: "Looks like you and André are
having fun building that road together." Or "I like
the way you held Megan's hand when she was
crying." You can teach young children that they
have the power to care for themselves, other people,
and the world.

Today
I'll notice when a child makes a difference.

April 5

**"We need many caring people in our lives.
We need to reweave the web that connects us,
so that we have a safety net when we slip."**
Louise Hart, Ph.D.

How many caring people do you have in your life?
Think about family, relatives, friends, neighbors,
coworkers, mentors, and members of your faith
community. All of these people are part of your
web—they're the strands that connect you, support
you, and protect you. Now think about who makes
up your child's web: family, relatives, teachers, caregivers, friends, and so on. Research has shown that
children who have a greater web of support have a
greater chance of success in life.

Today
I'll help build my child's web.

SUPPORT
ASSET #3: OTHER ADULT RELATIONSHIPS

April 6

"Experiences and sensations are learning."
Carla Hannaford, Ph.D.

For young children, learning isn't all in their heads—it's all in their senses. When we give babies a new flavor of baby food, we're giving them a different experience—one that they learn from. Taking toddlers or preschoolers to the zoo for the first time opens up a new world of sights, sounds, and smells. Whenever we give children experiences that engage one or more of their five senses, they learn something new. You can give children something different to smell, touch, taste, hear, or see each day.

Today
I'll provide new sensory experiences.

April 7

**"Children need to know they are
more important to us than anything they *do*."**
Jane Nelsen, Ed.D.

Your toddler throws a ball in the living room and
smashes your favorite vase. Most likely, you're
angry that the vase is broken and frustrated that
your toddler threw the ball indoors when you told
him or her not to. On the other hand, you're
relieved that your child's not hurt. Toddlers are
impulsive; they move fast, and they need constant
supervision. But they're also able to grasp that
their behavior has consequences. You can say, "I
need to take that ball away now. It's an outdoor
toy only." Your toddler will be upset, but you can
gently explain, "I don't like what you did, but I
still like *you*."

Today
I'll reassure my child after disciplining him or her.

BOUNDARIES AND EXPECTATIONS
ASSET #11: FAMILY BOUNDARIES

April 8

**"If you judge people,
you have no time to love them."**
Mother Teresa

When you're with children every day, it's hard not to choose favorites. Some children may seem sweeter, funnier, or more loving than others. On the flip side, some children may require you to be much more patient, tolerant, or understanding than you ever thought you could be. Through the years, you'll see children of different backgrounds, abilities, and temperaments. Give all of them your time and attention. No matter how they look or how they act, all children deserve the chance to be loved.

Today
I'll love children equally.

April 9

"Letters are great because they open communication between families and other adults involved in kids' lives."
Lynn Stambaugh

Encouragement and support are two of the most effective tools a teacher has. If you're a teacher or a caregiver, you may want to regularly send home encouraging notes to parents, telling of their children's progress. Parents will welcome news of their children's accomplishments—in fact, notes like these can really brighten a parent's day. You can write notes about a child's developing motor, verbal, or social skills; you may even want to offer suggestions for continuing this development at home. If you're a parent, notice something your child has learned in someone else's care—a song, a word, a dance—and write a note thanking that person for sharing this with your child.

Today
I'll write a note to a parent or caregiver.

April 10

"Running, sliding, climbing, and playing with balls are all important ways in which children learn."
Diane Trister Dodge

We sometimes make the mistake of forcing young children to learn new skills. We show them flash cards, have them practice counting to ten, or ask them to recite the alphabet. These activities stimulate learning, but so does *playing*. In fact, young children learn best while playing. Pretending, dressing up, running, jumping, and creating all build skills and confidence. Play is a stimulating activity—it should be a big part of each child's day.

Today
I'll let children learn through play.

April 11

"The family is the most significant place where faith development occurs."
Mark Holmen

In our families, we teach children what to have faith in and what not to have faith in. Our faith reveals what we think of the world, other people, and ourselves. If we believe it's important to help others, we may encourage each family member to give money to a congregation or a charity—even if it's just a few pennies from a young child. We may say prayers at daybreak, mealtime, or bedtime, go to weekly services, or celebrate religious holidays. What we do as a family teaches our children what to believe in—and how to develop a faith of their own.

Today
I'll notice what I'm teaching my children about faith.

April 12

**"It isn't hard to be good from time to time. . . .
What's tough is being good every day."**
Willie Mays

Integrity emerges slowly in young children (in fact, you may not see it until the elementary-school years). When children are toddlers or preschoolers, you can reinforce the message that it's important for everyone to do and be their best each day. Model integrity by being true to your word and keeping your promises. If you say you're going to do something for your children, such as take them outside to play after you've finished some work, do so in a reasonable time frame. Your children will see that they can depend on you and trust what you tell them.

Today
I'll be true to my word.

April 13

**"Though the world is a dangerous place,
it is also a safe place."**
Gavin de Becker

Most young children experience normal separation anxiety at some point. An infant may cry when handed over to the new baby-sitter; a toddler may cling to a parent while being dropped off at the childcare center; a preschooler may express misgivings about starting kindergarten. Separation fears need to be handled with care. If you're a parent, help your child feel more secure about these transitions by giving him or her a hug and leaving quickly (lingering only prolongs the anxiety). If you're a teacher or caregiver, help the child by welcoming him or her with a warm smile or caring hug. In group activities, assure children that everyone feels a little scared when their parents leave, but the feelings soon pass.

Today
I'll help a child feel safe and secure.

EMPOWERMENT
ASSET #10: SAFETY

April 14

**"The more you let your child do for himself,
the more capable he will feel."**
Robert Butterworth, Ph.D.

Children can take responsibility from an early age.
Some infants can hold their own bottle; older babies
can spoon food into their mouth. Some toddlers can
put on their own pants and socks (they may still
need help with shoes and shirts). Preschoolers can
lend a hand in the kitchen by tearing lettuce for a
salad and putting napkins beside each place setting.
Taking responsibility gives children a sense of
pride. When they accomplish a task, they feel good
about themselves and often want to do more.

Today

I'll give a child a simple task to feel proud of.

April 15

**"We particularly need a social commitment
to providing opportunities for meaningful roles
for young people."**
Elena O. Nightingale, M.D., Ph.D.

One person can make a difference in the life of a
child, but a whole group of people can do even
more. April is the Month of the Young Child, a time
for communities, childcare centers, preschools,
pediatric clinics, libraries, and neighborhoods to
celebrate young children. Display children's artwork in hallways and entrances; hang up photographs of all the children in your group; make
waiting areas more appealing to young children by
providing books or activities. This is a month to
reflect on what we've done for young children so
far and to consider what we might do for them in
the future.

Today
I'll celebrate the Month of the Young Child.

April 16

"Your education and imagination will carry you to places which you won't believe possible."
Ellison Onizuka

Young children often have big dreams and high hopes. They want to build the world's highest block tower; they want to ride a bike like the big kids do; they want to write their name and tie their shoes. They often get discouraged when their body or hands won't cooperate. And they may feel frustrated when they don't have the knowledge to do what they dream of. You can show young children that learning and practice are the keys to mastering new skills. Let children know that, in time, they'll be able to do what they imagine themselves doing and *more.*

Today
**I'll help a child understand
that learning takes time.**

April 17

"Students should be involved in the formation of classroom rules."
Edward Wynne and Kevin Ryan

Preschoolers are beginning to learn more about self-control; they have a better understanding of the consequences of their behavior. At this age, they can be given clear, simple rules while at school or in a childcare center: *Walk in the halls. Take turns and share. Keep your hands to yourself during circle time.* You may even want to ask the children in your group for help in making signs that post the rules. For example, they could put their handprints on a bathroom sign reading "Wash your hands." When children are part of the rule-making process, they're more likely to remember what they're supposed to do—and to remind others as well.

Today
I'll invite children to help with rules.

April 18

**"When we perform acts of kindness,
we get a wonderful feeling inside."**
Rabbi Harold Kushner, Ph.D.

Kindness is catching—when someone does something kind for you, you immediately want to return the favor, and when you *do,* you feel even better. Your family can practice acts of kindness every day—it's a wonderful way to teach your child about caring. To get started, invite your child to color a picture for Grandma or Grandpa, help you mail a letter to a faraway friend or relative, act as your kitchen helper while you make a special batch of soup for a loved one, or simply lavish some attention on the family pet. Your child will enjoy helping you spread a little kindness around.

Today

I'll do a kind act with my child.

April 19

"I remember loving sound
before I ever took a music lesson.
And so we make our lives by what we love."
John Cage

Some young children naturally take to a creative
activity—it captures their heart right away. Maybe
they love painting, tumbling, building, or drum-
ming on pots and pans; maybe they're inspired by
puppets, music, or books. Other children need more
time and experience to figure out what they enjoy
doing. You can help by providing lots of opportunities for creative exploration. Make sure your
home or classroom is filled with books, paper, art
supplies, blocks, and music. Encourage singing
and creative movement. You can even have children help you make homemade sock puppets
or musical instruments.

Today
I'll help children find creative activities they love.

April 20

**"Communication is only half about content.
The other half is about process."**

Ann L. Weber, Ph.D.

Why do you confide in some people but not others?
Most likely, you confide only in people you've come
to trust—people who are open and approachable.
Someone who acted gruff or in a rush when you
needed to talk isn't someone you'd be likely to go to
again. Young children feel this way, too. They learn
about communication based on the feedback they
receive when trying to communicate with adults.
They'll talk with someone they feel safe around.
They'll talk with a willing listener. They'll talk with
someone who values what they say.

Today

**I'll notice how well I speak and listen
to my children.**

April 21

**"Hold your head high, stick your chest out.
You can make it. It gets dark sometimes,
but the morning comes."**
Jesse Jackson

Young children are familiar with frustration. They struggle with each new milestone: taking their first steps, giving up a pacifier, drinking from a cup, learning to use the potty, figuring out how to button, snap, zip, or tie. During these skill-building times, young children may become so frustrated that they want to give up and revert to what's familiar. They may shout, "No!" and resist learning a new way. Parents and caregivers can help by staying calm and refusing to get into a power struggle. Remember not to push young children too hard.

Today
I'll be patient with a frustrated child.

April 22

"Read all you can lay your hands on, from the label
on the ketchup bottles to literature's masters.
The rewards of reading never diminish
and continue forever to broaden your horizons."

Helen Ganz

Some parents read to children even before they're born; others read aloud to infants, particularly during those 2 A.M. feedings. Newborns and infants benefit from read-aloud time, even if they don't understand the meaning of the words. They enjoy a soothing voice, quiet time, and snuggling—all of which reading aloud can provide. Find books that have a touch-and-feel quality (*Pat the Bunny* by Dorothy Kunhardt is an old favorite), so babies can touch each page as you read. When you make books a part of everyday life from the start, young children learn that reading is pleasurable and important.

Today
I'll read to a baby.

April 23

**"I started introducing myself
to people I didn't know who live on my street
and to the merchants who run the businesses
in my hometown."**
Susan Ungaro

Susan Ungaro—the editor of *Family Circle* magazine—realized that, in her community, she saw the same faces over and over, but she didn't know people's names. She decided to take the initiative and reach out—she began introducing herself to neighbors, shop owners, cashiers, and other people she came in contact with. As she began to learn people's names, they began to learn hers. Sometimes *you* have to be the one to make the effort. You can get to know your neighbors better: learning people's faces is the first step, and the next is learning their names.

Today
I'll introduce myself to a neighbor.

SUPPORT
ASSET #4: CARING NEIGHBORHOOD

April 24

**"Living is a constant process of deciding
what we are going to do."**
José Ortega y Gasset

When you give preschoolers the power to choose,
you help build their decision-making skills. At this
age, children like to pick out their own clothes—an
excellent opportunity to show them how to plan
ahead and make choices. Start the night before,
allowing preschoolers plenty of time to choose.
Don't be surprised if they opt for shorts in winter or
a turtleneck in summer; guide their clothing choices
to make sure they're appropriate for the weather.
Otherwise, give preschoolers some leeway. They
may end up with a clashing outfit and mismatched
socks—but they've made a choice they're happy
with, and that counts for a lot!

Today
I'll let my preschooler decide what to wear.

April 25

"I got dizzy from laughing, lost my breath from laughing. My stomach hurt from laughing. Tears ran from my eyes."
Michael Dorris

If you're the parent of a baby, you may often feel worn out and worked up. Babies demand so much care—constant feeding, burping, diapering, bathing, and dressing. If you feel frazzled, don't take your feelings out on your baby; try to see the humor in the situation instead. He just flung strained peas on the wall? Laugh about it! She's learned to unwrap the entire toilet-tissue dispenser? Take a photo and share it with friends. Humor is a great tension-buster. (P.S. April is National Humor Month.)

Today
I'll laugh when tension mounts.

SOCIAL COMPETENCIES
ASSET #36: PEACEFUL CONFLICT RESOLUTION

April 26

**"Volunteering is an activity
most likely to be cultivated in childhood."**
Researchers at Independent Sector (IS)

Independent Sector is an organization that works to promote, strengthen, and advance the nonprofit and philanthropic community. In a study to explore the volunteering and giving habits of teenagers and adults, IS researchers found that the majority of teenage volunteers first began serving others before they turned twelve. Consider choosing one day a month for your family or childcare center to volunteer. Or give spontaneously: have your child add an extra can of food to your shopping cart to bring to a food shelf, or create handmade cards to take or send to the children's wing of a hospital. If you teach children to serve others at an early age, you'll help form a good habit that's likely to stay.

Today
I'll help a child to volunteer.

April 27

**"I believe there's an inner power
that makes winners or losers.
And the winners are the ones
who really listen to the truth of their hearts."**
Sylvester Stallone

What drives you? What speaks to your heart? What gives your life purpose? Being in touch with what's important to you helps you better define your interests, passions, hopes, and dreams. Share your sense of purpose with your young child; demonstrate your beliefs through your actions. For example, if you love to run, explain this to your child: "Running helps my body feel good. It keeps me healthy and happy. Someday, I'd like to run in a race with other grown-ups." Find a way to include your child in your favorite activity, if possible.

Today

I'll help my child see what gives my life purpose.

April 28

"One of the most wonderful aspects of taking a class together is that it will strengthen the bond between you."
Beth Teitelman

Many communities offer low-cost classes for parents and their young children. You may be able to take a class in music, movement, or infant massage, for example. If you're interested, see what's available through community education, the parks and recreation department, YMCA/YWCA, or ECFE (Early Childhood and Family Education) programs. These classes can help you and your child learn something new—and get closer, too.

Today
I'll sign up for a class with my child.

April 29

"I have lots of fun with my daddy."
Camera Ashe (age five)

Young children spend most of their time with a parent, and this relationship teaches them something about friendship. Camera Ashe loved playing a game called Big Hug, Little Hug; Big Kiss, Little Kiss with her dad, tennis star Arthur Ashe. They also climbed trees in the park and sat in the sun and sang. Through these fun times together, Camera learned about positive interaction with a special person in her life. As she grew, she was able to move beyond this primary relationship into positive relationships with friends. Children get more involved in friendships as they grow. You can get to know their friends and ask questions like, "What's fun about being with each other? What do the two of you like to do?"

Today
I'll have fun with my child.

April 30

"Always speak the truth—think before you speak."
Lewis Carroll

April 30 is National Honesty Day. To celebrate, the day's organizers accept nominations of honest people and companies, and then give awards to the winners. If your community were to give out these awards each year, which caregivers, preschool teachers, parents, and advocates for children would you nominate and why? Which organizations for children (such as childcare centers, preschools, congregational nurseries, community-education programs, and child clubs) would you recommend and why? Celebrate this day by thanking each individual or organization that came to mind.

Today
I'll say thanks in a letter or in person.

May 1

"April showers bring May flowers."
Mother Goose

Little Boy Blue, Little Bo Peep, Humpty Dumpty . . . these classic characters, and the rhymes that describe them, were created long ago but are still a vital part of children's literature. Today is Mother Goose Day, so celebrate the nursery rhymes and songs that have entertained young children for generations. Even as adults, we often remember with fondness our favorite Mother Goose poems, songs, and rhymes—and the illustrations that went with them. As you introduce Mother Goose to young children, you can rediscover these classics and remember which ones you loved best.

Today
I'll read Mother Goose to a child.

May 2

"We should consider touch as essential as diet and exercise are to the growth and well-being of children."
Tiffany Field, Ph.D.

Researcher Tiffany Field, director of the Touch Research Institute at the University of Miami School of Medicine, found that infants gained more weight and were more alert and active when they were touched on a regular basis. All young children benefit from being touched; it's a wonderful way to show your love and support. You can cuddle young children, rock them, hold them, carry them, or let them sit on your lap. You can stroke their hair, rub their back, or hold their hand. You can show caring through both gentle and playful touches.

Today
I'll show my support through touch.

May 3

**"Learning to experience and control states
of intense emotion is one of the crucial tasks
of growing up."**
James M. Herzog, M.D.

Teaching young children about handling emotions
can be of the most difficult tasks for parents and
caregivers. Toddlers and preschoolers are prone to
temper tantrums, crying spells, and aggressive
behavior such as hitting, kicking, or biting—these
emotional outbursts are hard on both adults *and*
children. What can you do? Allow young children
to express their emotions; affirm what they're feeling, and then show appropriate ways to act. You
might say, "It's okay to get mad, but it's not okay to
kick," while bringing the child outdoors to run off
some of the excess energy that anger produces. This
message acknowledges that strong emotions are
normal and offers a positive way to cope.

Today
I'll help a child deal with strong emotions.

SOCIAL COMPETENCIES
ASSET #33: INTERPERSONAL SKILLS

May 4

**"While it may take a village to raise a child,
it takes responsible and caring adults
to make a nurturing village."**
Kenneth Edelin

The people of Nampa, Idaho, have been working for years to improve their community, and in 1993, they added a goal of becoming asset builders for their children and youth. Nampa now has a community center that hosts cultural and recreational activities for children and families with diverse interests and backgrounds. The community also partnered with organizations to create programs in childcare, reading skills, and computer education. If you'd like to make your community a better place for children but you're not sure where to start, take a closer look at Nampa, Idaho, or one of the other 600 healthy communities for children at this Web site: *www.search-institute.org*. You'll find information and tools for improving children's lives.

Today
I'll do my part to nurture children in my community.

May 5

> **"Cherish and preserve the ethnic
> and cultural diversity that nourishes
> and strengthens this community—and this nation."**
> *César Chávez*

May 5 is Cinco de Mayo, a day to celebrate and commemorate Latino culture. In Mexico, in parts of the U.S., and in other places of the world, Cinco de Mayo celebrations highlight food, entertainment, dancing, and arts and crafts. Whatever your children's racial identities or ethnic heritages may be, find ways to help them feel proud of who they are. For example, you might give young children dolls and toys that reflect their heritages or provide books that positively portray people of different ethnicities. You can also affirm the many different races and cultures around you to show young children that you value, appreciate, and celebrate *everyone*.

Today
I'll celebrate diversity.

May 6

"Neighbors should discuss ways to make sure children are aware of the rules."
Stephanie Mann

You turn your back only for a second—and discover that your toddler has flattened a neighbor's flowers with his tricycle. Your preschooler reaches out to pet a neighbor's dog—only to get her hand nipped. Spending time outdoors among friends and neighbors is important for young children, but safety needs to be a priority. The best time to talk about neighborhood rules is *before* something happens. Show young children how to respect other people's property and belongings; for example, let them see that flowers and bushes must be handled with care. Explain that children should never approach an animal—even a friendly looking pet—without the okay of an adult.

Today
I'll talk about neighborhood rules.

May 7

"There's only one corner of the universe you can be certain of improving, and that's your own self."
Aldous Huxley

As children grow, one important truth they discover is that the person they have the most influence over is themselves. Preschoolers, for example, are learning to become more independent; they test themselves and take pride in each new accomplishment. You can help build preschoolers' self-esteem by giving them opportunities to take care of their own needs. Put toys and art supplies within reach, so preschoolers have access to activities; allow preschoolers to set their own place at lunch or pour themselves a drink from a small pitcher; let them choose books they're interested in from the library. Self-reliance and support are building blocks for self-esteem.

Today
I'll help my child be more independent.

May 8

**"Children respond to the expectations
of their environment."**
William Grier

If we don't tend the flowers we've planted, they wither and fade. Living things need good care; they flourish in positive environments. As parents and caregivers, we have a responsibility to see that our schools and childcare centers are inviting places for young children. Children learn by doing—they need opportunities for hands-on learning through art, music, creative movement, cooking, and dramatic play. These learning experiences—and the environments that support them—ensure that children have the best chance to bloom and grow.

Today

**I'll support hands-on activities
in our childcare center or preschool.**

May 9

**"The difficult we do immediately.
The impossible takes a little longer."**
U.S. Corps of Engineers

Young children need the chance to know and observe motivated, successful adults—including you. Show them that you want to succeed at home, at work, in the community, and in volunteer activities. Model a "can do" attitude to prove to the children in your care that positive thinking and persistence can lead to success. Children notice when you're motivated and enthusiastic. They feel more excited in your presence, and they learn to take pleasure in each new task or accomplishment.

Today
I'll be motivated.

May 10

"True peace is not merely the absence of tension; it is the presence of justice."
Martin Luther King Jr.

With preschoolers, you may often hear cries of "That's not fair!" Children this age are beginning to understand fairness, and they get upset when something seems unjust. When the tension mounts and you hear "That's not fair," you can talk to your child about these feelings. You might ask, "How do you feel when someone treats you this way?" and "What can we do to make this more fair?" Use this opportunity to discuss ways to treat all people more fairly and equally.

Today
I'll talk about fairness.

May 11

"They can because they think they can."
Virgil

People (even little ones) love to hear about others who have done "big things." For example, toddlers get excited when they hear about preschoolers who can do somersaults; preschoolers enjoy thinking about how they'll soon be big enough to tie their shoes or ride the school bus. Telling stories of what other children have done is one way to encourage young children to stretch and grow. You can share stories of their older siblings, cousins, or neighbors; you can show books or magazines that have pictures of real kids in action. Help children understand that trying new things—sometimes over and over and over—is the best way to succeed.

Today
I'll help a child stretch.

May 12

"All children are born ready and willing to learn."
Carnegie Task Force on Learning

While all children are born willing to learn, some lose their natural curiosity and enthusiasm too early in life. To foster a lifelong love of learning, the Carnegie Task Force says that children need (1) high-quality preschools or childcare programs that prepare them for elementary school, (2) involved parents and caregivers who create home environments that foster learning, and (3) communities that provide supportive programs for parents and high-quality educational opportunities for young children. We can encourage children to learn by starting where we are: in our homes, in our childcare centers, in our preschools, in our communities. When we give children stimulating activities they enjoy, they learn—and they keep on learning.

Today
I'll provide stimulating learning experiences.

May 13

"You have to be loose enough to do some things on the spur of the moment, or life isn't fun."
Nick Stinnett, Ph.D.

Today, even young children may have over-scheduled lives, as we find ourselves rushing from place to place and activity to activity, with our children in tow. But when our calendars are full, we may forget the importance of simply spending time together as a family and doing things on the spur of the moment. Instead of arranging back-to-back activities this weekend, take a mini-vacation by hanging out at home. Don't cook, clean, or organize—just have fun! Camp out in a homemade fort, make s'mores in the microwave, and play games with your child. Young children love surprises, adventure, and spontaneity.

Today
I'll be spontaneous.

May 14

**"Role models can be black.
Role models can be white."**
Colin Powell

Role models can be *any* color. When you think about finding role models for your child, you may naturally consider people who are successful and inspiring. You can broaden your search by looking for role models who are from diverse ethnicities and cultures as well. When young children get to know people of different races and backgrounds, their view of the world expands. Give children access to many kinds of role models—black, white, young, old, single, married, wealthy, not-so-wealthy.

Today
I'll consider what makes a good role model.

May 15

**"A baby is God's opinion
that the world should go on."**
Carl Sandburg

People make a fuss over newborns because they're tiny and adorable; they also represent hope, innocence, and new beginnings. Babies inspire the feeling that we live in a world full of goodness and fresh starts. If you're a parent or caregiver of a newborn or an infant, savor these joyful feelings. If you begin to feel tired or overwhelmed by the responsibility of caring for a baby, find a way to recharge. Ask for help, take a break, slow down, or do a little less than you'd planned. When you keep focusing on positive feelings, you'll be more hopeful and relaxed.

Today
I'll see hope for the future when I look at an infant.

POSITIVE IDENTITY
ASSET #40: POSITIVE VIEW OF PERSONAL FUTURE

May 16

**"The willingness to accept responsibility
for one's own life is the source
from which self-respect springs."**
Joan Didion

With our first experience caring for a young child, whether as a first-time parent or a first-time caregiver, our circle of responsibility widens. We're responsible for our own lives *and* for the life of a child. The larger circle of responsibility can feel overwhelming, but when we accept it, we grow — and so does our self-respect. We come to realize that a young child is depending on us to be the one in charge, the one who makes things safe and secure. Knowing that someone so young relies on us — and that we can meet those needs — is one of life's sweetest rewards.

Today
I'll embrace the responsibility of caring for a child.

May 17

**"When you clench your fist,
no one can put anything in your hand,
nor can your hand pick up anything."**
Alex Haley

Preschoolers are old enough to understand the idea
that our bodies have a language of their own: our
bodies react to how we're feeling and send messages to us and to other people. Ask each child what
anger feels like: "Does your heart beat faster?"
"Does your face feel hot?" "Do you feel tight and
tense?" "Do you clench your fists?" You can show
young children that clenched fists don't open
easily — and that you can't hold hands with someone
who's making a fist. Help them see that anger
doesn't have to lead to fighting. When they feel their
bodies signaling anger, they can take a deep breath
and calm down. They can ask an adult for help.

Today
I'll teach the warning signs of anger.

SOCIAL COMPETENCIES
ASSET #36: PEACEFUL CONFLICT RESOLUTION

May 18

"My father used to play with my brother and me in the yard. Mother would come out and say, 'You're tearing up the grass.' 'We're not raising grass,' my dad would reply. 'We're raising boys.'"
Harmon Killebrew

When you start having kids, you start having a messier home—it's inevitable, so it's best to get used to the idea. Young children leave sticky handprints on the windows and walls; they spill juice on the rugs; they may even spit up on the furniture. Instead of getting upset, accept the mess as part of the challenge of raising children. It may help to set up a separate play area where your preschoolers are free to spread out their toys, or to take toddlers outside when they're involved in a particularly messy activity. Giving young children room to be themselves is an important boundary you can set for yourself as a parent.

Today
I won't get concerned about a mess.

May 19

> "We sow the seeds and set out the plants in the soil, and watch the rainbow grow."
>
> *Lois Ehlert*

In her picture book *Planting a Rainbow,* Lois Ehlert shows the colorful rainbow that children can plant: red roses, orange poppies, yellow daffodils, green ferns, blue morning glories, and purple pansies. Now that spring's here, you may want to spend time in a garden with a young child, teaching him or her about the wonders of nature. Besides the rainbow of flowers, you might plant a rainbow of vegetables: red radishes, orange carrots, yellow squash, green peas, blueberries, and purple eggplants. You'll both enjoy digging in the dirt to make things grow.

Today

I'll spend time exploring nature with a child.

May 20

"Your youngster may be so totally preoccupied with a book, a bug, or project that she won't hear you say it's time for a meal."
Sally Yahnke Walker, Ph.D.

When young children are engaged in learning, they may become so absorbed that they seem to ignore the world around them. They may not hear you or notice you; they may seem as if they're in another world. Don't take this as a sign that something's wrong with your child's hearing or ability to understand you; more likely, your child is completely engrossed in an activity. You can encourage your child by providing plenty of interesting experiences and activities, and allowing uninterrupted exploration. Once your child's interest wanes, you might say, "Wow, you really were enjoying yourself. What did you like about that activity?"

Today
I'll let my child play or learn without interruption.

May 21

"All kids need is a little help, a little hope, and somebody who believes in them."
Earvin "Magic" Johnson

Having one person who believes in you is powerful; having more than one person who believes in you is even better! Who believed in you when you were young? Who cared for you and supported you? Who helped you and gave you a sense of hope? Today, thank that special someone and make a promise to be the same kind of person for a child in your life. You can show support in many ways: spend an hour one-on-one with a young child, take him or her to the park or a children's museum, or play a game and do an art project together.

Today
I'll be someone a child can count on.

SUPPORT
ASSET #3: OTHER ADULT RELATIONSHIPS

May 22

"Courage is the only thing."
Winston Churchill

Sometimes, parents and caregivers are so stressed out or overwhelmed that they forget to treat young children with the respect and care they need. If you see an adult who has reached his or her limit with a child, what can you do? It takes courage to step in and help, but you can do so in a way that doesn't create a conflict—if you focus on the child, not on the adult's behavior. You might say, "I see the baby is crying and that you need a break. May I hold him for a few minutes while you rest?" By speaking up in a helpful way, you can comfort the child and the adult.

Today

I'll help an adult—and a child—who needs me.

May 23

"A hero is someone who has given his or her life to something bigger than oneself."
Joseph Campbell

If you ask preschoolers what a hero is, they may describe someone with superhuman powers who can fly and battle the "bad guys." You can explain that everyday people are the *real* heroes in life — the ones who help others not because they have special "powers" but because they care about people. If young children seem fascinated by cartoon heroes who kick, throw punches, and fight, point out heroes who act in more positive ways. You might say, "Did you know that Uncle Mario helps dogs and cats at the animal shelter?" Or "Dr. Green works hard to help all the children who see her to get better when they're sick."

Today
I'll talk about real-life heroes.

May 24

"Imagination is the highest kite one can fly."
Lauren Bacall

Every preschooler can have fun painting or drawing, but what about helping them take these activities even further? You might provide unusual supplies (feathers, seashells, beads, corks, spools) that young children can paste or glue onto their pictures for added dimension and interest. As they create, you can ask them "what if" questions to further stimulate their imaginations: "What if this fish swam in orange juice instead of water?" "What if feathers were growing on your body?" "What if the sun you're drawing had a necklace? What might it look like?" Help their imaginations take flight!

Today
I'll help children think in new directions.

May 25

**"Rather than think of all the reasons
why you can't be active, come up
with some creative ways to help out
within the confines of your schedule."**
Ginny Markell, President of the National PTA

We all have busy schedules or deadlines to meet.
Yet, as parents, we need to make time to support our
children, even when they're away from home.
Whether your child is involved in a preschool, childcare center, congregational nursery, or class, you can
set aside time to show your support for this place
and all of the children in it. Perhaps you might volunteer for an hour once a month to read stories to
the children; maybe you could organize a special
activity or help decorate the room for a celebration.
Ask your child's caregiver how you can get
involved.

Today
I'll find out how I can help.

May 26

**"Children seek the opportunity
to be in charge of themselves."**
Paul Tieger and Barbara Barron-Tieger

If toddlers or babies get hurt, it's best to rush to their aid and soothe them quickly: these young children learn about their personal power by having their needs met right away. But by the time they're preschoolers, they may want to choose how to be comforted. Some preschoolers like to be cuddled when they're hurt, others don't; some preschoolers think of an antiseptic as "scratch medicine" and like to have it applied to their wounds, while others see that as another "owie" and scream even more. And some preschoolers insist on having an adhesive bandage put on *any* kind of hurt, including a bruise or an invisible scrape. You can pay attention to how each child needs to be soothed—this helps a child feel cared for and empowered.

Today
I'll let my preschooler choose how to be comforted.

May 27

"Don't come back! Until I say so."
Ed Emberley

Toddlers and preschoolers often feel scared of monsters and other imaginary dangers. When you give a young child the power to take charge of such fears, he or she can more easily resist them. One parent encouraged her preschooler to draw his monster, and then rip up the picture and throw it away (to get rid of the monster). Another parent taught her daughter to shout "Go away!" to any monsters she was frightened of. Ed Emberley's book *Go Away, Big Green Monster!* is a good one to share with young children who have monster fears; it empowers children to tell their fears to go away, page by page.

Today
I'll help my child deal with a fear.

SOCIAL COMPETENCIES
ASSET #35: RESISTANCE SKILLS

May 28

"Aquellos son ricos que tienen amigos."
"When there are friends, there is wealth."
Southwestern Spanish proverb

Our friends enrich our lives through their caring, encouragement, and support—providing us with wealth that can't be measured in dollars or cents. Even children as young as three to five need friends—but how many? Some children are more introverted and prefer quieter activities with fewer people; other children are extroverted and love being part of a group. Take a cue from your child—what is his or her preference and temperament? If your child enjoys spending time mainly with one close friend, encourage this friendship by having frequent play dates. If your child likes to be among lots of other children, take him or her to a public park or children's play group as often as you can.

Today
I'll think about my child's unique social needs.

May 29

**"Mirror, mirror, on the wall,
who is the fairest one of all?"**
The Queen in Snow White

A mirror is a fascinating tool for young children—they love to see their own reflections and to discover what their faces and bodies can do. If you stand in front of a mirror with a baby in your arms, he will probably smile or bat at the glass. If you hang a full-length mirror in a toddler's or preschooler's play area, she will use it while playing dress-up or trying out new creative movements. You can gather young children before a mirror to see who can make the most outlandish faces: open your eyes wide, scrunch up your features, stick out your tongues. Together, you can practice expressions that range from silly to serious.

Today
I'll have fun with a child in front of a mirror.

COMMITMENT TO LEARNING
ASSET #23: STIMULATING ACTIVITY AND HOMEWORK

May 30

**"Schools must be places
where children are free from fear
and free to learn."**
New York State United Teachers report

Some preschools and childcare centers aren't as safe as they need to be; they may have wiring that's not up to code or contain toxins like lead paint. When young children feel afraid or sense that they're in danger (in response to how the adults around them act), they're not as able to learn, thrive, and grow. All children who are involved in out-of-home care need to be in environments that keep the danger and fear out—and let safety and learning in. The first step is becoming aware of the possible hazards. And then, by advocating for children and making changes where needed, we can create safer places for children outside the home.

Today

I'll consider whether my child is in a safe place.

May 31

"If you can dream it, you can do it."
Walt Disney

Dreams stretch children and help them believe in themselves. One young girl imagined being a train conductor, and her parents took this dream seriously. They brought her to a local train station to watch the trains; they also took a train ride, and the conductor put his hat on the little girl's head and called her his "junior conductor." This inspired her to draw trains and look at books about them. Her parents helped teach her that dreams can lead her to the places she wants to go in life. How might you teach this to your own child?

Today
I'll help my child imagine possibilities.

June 1

"There is a call to us, a call of service—
that we join with others
to try to make things better in this world."
Dorothy Day

June 1–7 is International Volunteer's Week. Young children enjoy helping others—it gives them a sense of pride. You can participate in service projects that produce immediate results, so young children can see the power of their own actions. For example, you might have them draw pictures for residents at a center for senior citizens and deliver the pictures in person; the children will feel good when they see the smiles on the residents' faces and hear their thank yous. Young children gain a better understanding of the world—and their power to make it a better place—when you give them a chance to serve in a way that's meaningful to them.

Today
I'll find a way to let children help others.

June 2

**"You don't just luck into things. . . .
You build step by step,
whether it's friendships or opportunities."**
Barbara Bush

Luck only gets you so far—planning is essential to building the life you want for you and your children. If you don't already do so, consider using a calendar and to-do lists to help you better plan your days. While these tools may seem obvious, they work. Get into the habit of writing down goals and moving toward them day by day, so you feel more in control of your life. You can model these skills for your children, so they learn early on about the importance of making plans and decisions.

Today
I'll get better organized.

June 3

"Reunions provide a chance for members to achieve a deeper appreciation for the family."
Joy Hong

Summer is a popular time for family reunions and gatherings. Often, these events are geared mainly toward adults and older kids. In the process of planning the food and making sure everyone can come, it's easy to overlook the young children who will be there. Next time you plan a gathering, be sure to include games, activities, or entertainment that will stimulate the toddlers and preschoolers who attend. (You may even want to ask them ahead of time what they would enjoy doing.) This ensures that everyone at the get-together will have a memorable time.

Today
I'll include children in my plans.

June 4

"La verdad, aunque severa, es amiga verdadera."
"The truth, although severe, is a true friend."
Southwestern Spanish proverb

Young children watch us closely, and as they do, our words and actions become powerful teachers. When you lie or stretch the truth in front of a young child, he or she gets the impression that dishonesty is acceptable. If you realize you've lied, take a moment to explain to your child why you acted this way. You might say, "When I said I couldn't take you to the park because of the weather, that wasn't the truth. I'm feeling tired, so I made an excuse. I was wrong to do that." When you admit what you've done, you teach the importance of telling the truth.

Today
I'll admit if I haven't been honest.

June 5

**"If you want your child to grow up
with positive feelings about religion,
don't expect him to sit quietly for a long time
in uncomfortable clothing at religious services."**
Ava Siegler, Ph.D.

Many congregations are working to make their services more inviting to children. For example, some offer "busy bags" that young children can play with quietly as they listen. Others provide children's worship bulletins that include pages to color and activities to try. Still, some toddlers and preschoolers can't help but wiggle or make noise in quiet places. As they grow older, they'll learn to settle down. You might help by collecting used picture books to make available to the young children in your congregation.

Today
I'll be patient with a squirmy child.

June 6

**"Children are the purpose of life.
We were once children and someone cared for us.
Now it's our time to care."**
Cree elder

When we were children, others cared for us. The adults who raised us made sure we had the basics: food, shelter, clothing, medical care. They believed in us; they helped us learn and grow. Now, as adults, it's our turn to care—as parents or as caregivers. We can give the young children in our lives the basics they need and more: we can teach them, play with them, guide them, help them, nurture them, and care for them. In this way, we continue the circle of support that started when we were young.

Today
I'll let a child depend on me.

June 7

"Neighborhood fun seems to spawn a powerful sense of community."
Teri Keough

Summer is an ideal time to connect with your neighbors—the warmer weather means more time outdoors and more kids around. Some neighborhoods hold special summertime events to help foster a sense of community. For example, people may organize block parties or get-to-know-you socials where food, games, and sports are the featured entertainment; kids may even parade around the block riding in strollers, on tricycles, or on bikes. While these events require effort to plan, they bring people together. This summer (or any other time of year), you may want to help organize one of these events to meet more people. If you can't help with the planning, make time to attend with your family.

Today
I'll look into a neighborhood event.

June 8

**"One of the most important factors
in a child's success in school
is the degree to which his or her parents
are actively involved in the child's education."**
James Coleman and Thomas Hoffer

Researcher Joyce Epstein says that parents can participate in their children's education in six major ways. They can (1) enhance their parenting skills, (2) improve school-home communication, (3) volunteer at school, (4) help children learn at home, (5) participate in school decisions, and (6) encourage businesses to strengthen schools. Doing one thing is a start—but doing all six is the key. If your child isn't in childcare or preschool right now, you can focus on numbers one and four above.

Today
I'll know that my involvement is crucial.

June 9

**"I guess it's better to be who you are.
Turns out people like you best that way, anyway."**
***Big Bird**, from* **Sesame Street**

What do young children need more than anything? Unconditional love. They need to be loved just for who they are—not for who you expect them to be. Whether your child is an infant, a toddler, or a preschooler, you can demonstrate that you love him or her unconditionally, through your words and actions. You can hold and cuddle your child, say "I love you" frequently, and be patient and supportive as your child grows. Honor what's unique about your child to nurture his or her self-esteem.

Today
I'll show unconditional love.

June 10

**"If you find that your child is constantly
getting into trouble, the problem may not be
that she needs more discipline
but that the environment is wrong for her."**
Burton L. White, Ph.D.

If a crawling baby pulls himself up and starts eating
the soil of an indoor plant, it's time to move the
plant—or the baby. If a toddler opens a cabinet full
of cleaning products, this is a sign that the door
should have a childproof latch; you might distract
her with a toy while you secure the cabinet. Moving
a child out of danger, removing forbidden objects,
or redirecting a child to another activity are the best
solutions to these problems—instead of using discipline or loudly saying no. As children get older,
they're better able to learn about boundaries and
the meaning of no. Until then, it's our job as adults
to watch for danger and keep young children safe.

Today
I'll gently redirect a child.

BOUNDARIES AND EXPECTATIONS
ASSET #12: OUT-OF-HOME BOUNDARIES

June 11

> **"Children learn best when teachers order the environment to provide kids with interesting materials and new ideas to explore."**
> *Rebecca Marcon, Ph.D.*

Many childcare providers and preschool teachers create learning centers for children. Typical learning centers (or stations) may include a dramatic play area complete with costumes, shoes, and hats; a mini-kitchen with child-sized appliances, tables, and plastic food; a reading area with books; or an art section full of crayons, paints, paper, and play dough. Young children respond to these organized environments and enjoy exploring and experimenting in them. You can set up a play area in your home much the same way, organizing the toys and activities by their theme or their use. This makes playtime more stimulating—and simplifies cleanup, too.

Today
I'll organize my child's play area.

June 12

**"If you can walk, you can dance.
If you can talk, you can sing."**
Zimbabwe proverb

Creativity is about jumping in. Spend time with children doing what they do: dance, sing, color, scribble, doodle, draw. Don't judge the quality or wonder if this is time well spent. (Who cares if you stumble when you dance or hit a wrong note when you sing? Who'll notice if your art isn't museum worthy?) Unleash your creative side. Come out to play.

Today
I'll be creative with a child.

June 13

"Any pain is our pain: That's the root of tolerance."
Steven Spielberg

Teaching cultural competence to young children involves showing them that people are similar, even though they may look different or have unique ways of speaking, dressing, eating, and playing. Tolerance begins with an understanding that each person is an individual with feelings and needs. If your child seems disapproving of a child from another culture or expresses distaste for something that makes that child "different," you can help encourage tolerance. You might say, "Why do you feel that way about her? How do you think she feels when you say that? People are different in some ways, and the same in other ways. We can get to know others and like them, even if they're a little different from us."

Today
I'll help my child be more sensitive to others.

June 14

**"My favorite thing was going to neighbors
and having them give me pennies."**
Joseph Siegel (age five)

Joseph Siegel was one of thirty children in a New York City preschool who went on a mission to collect pennies to help others. By saving their pennies and asking people they knew to donate money, this group of three- to five-year-olds gathered 260,000 pennies—a total of $2,600! The children celebrated by eating pizza and talking about how to use their money to serve others. They voted not only to help homeless people and teen mothers and their babies, but also to fund children's art classes at a local museum. What could a group of young children in your area do, with help from you?

Today
I'll encourage children to serve others.

June 15

**"We must first explore
our own feelings about sexuality
and become more comfortable with them."**
Anne C. Bernstein, Ph.D.

Preschoolers may begin to ask questions about sexuality; some of these questions may take parents by surprise or even embarrass them. When asked, it's best to give simple, honest answers—this helps young children to gain healthy sexual attitudes and beliefs. If you'd like to better prepare yourself for what you might say if your child asks specific questions, take a look at Anne C. Bernstein's book *Flight of the Stork,* which discusses what children understand about reproduction at each age.

Today
I'll be responsive to children's questions.

June 16

"If you are a parent, recognize that it is
the most important calling and rewarding challenge
you have. What you do every day, what you say
and how you act, will do more to shape the future
of America than any other factor."
Marian Wright Edelman

Who has the most influence in the life of a child?
The parent. Young children observe, imitate, and
model their parents—this is how they learn about
the world and themselves. "The bottom line is that
children need to know that they can count on their
parents," says Byron Egeland of the Institute of
Child Development at the University of Minnesota.
As a parent, you are your children's most important
role model—the one they'll count on for a lifetime.

Today
I'll recognize the important role I play as a parent.

BOUNDARIES AND EXPECTATIONS
ASSET #14: ADULT ROLE MODELS

June 17

"Go and talk things over. Words can do magic."
Leo Lionni

Leo Lionni's children's book *Six Crows* tells of a conflict between a farmer and a group of hungry crows. When the crop almost dies because of the fighting, a wise owl encourages the two sides to talk and create a peaceful solution. Stories like this one are an ideal way to teach young children about peaceful conflict resolution. You can find other books that show how peaceful words and actions lead to solutions; spend some time at your local library browsing among the shelves with your child.

Today
I'll read a story that teaches a lesson.

June 18

**"You can do anything with children
if you only play with them."**
Otto von Bismarck

You may wonder how you can develop positive family communication if your child is too young to talk or understand much of what you say. There are other ways to communicate besides using words. Get down on the floor with your baby or toddler and make eye contact. Play, smile, laugh, make funny faces, gesture with your hands, hum, and touch your child. He or she will respond, and that's when communication takes place.

Today
I'll communicate with my child at his or her level.

June 19

"Surround yourself only with people who are going to lift you higher."
Oprah Winfrey

Relationships can lift you up or pull you down. Some people inspire you, help you feel good about yourself, and boost your energy, while others do the opposite. Surround yourself with people who lift you and your child higher—who help both of you stretch and grow. But don't stop there. Ask yourself how *you* can be a person who helps lift a child higher. In what ways might you be a source of support?

Today
I'll help my child find inspiration in another adult.

June 20

"Share and share alike."
Anonymous

When a popular new toy arrives on the scene, each child will want the chance to hold it, enjoy it, and spend time with it. Some preschools and childcare centers have created charts to help organize who plays with a popular item—each child usually gets five or ten minutes with a favored toy before giving it to someone else. You can try this at home if your children are at odds over certain toys, dolls, books, or activities. Let each child have a chance with the toy for a short, specified period of time (you may even want to set a timer that buzzes or beeps when the time's up). Once children get used to the new rules, they often come to enjoy the role of handing off the toy to the next person. Taking turns this way teaches children a valuable lesson about sharing.

Today
I'll let every child have a turn.

June 21

> **"Dream the biggest dream for yourself.
> Hold the highest vision of life for yourself."**
> *Duke Ellington*

At times, we get weighed down by our daily responsibilities. We think about our jobs, our chores, our bills, our children's needs. But as we focus on day-to-day life, we may lose sight of the bigger picture: our vision for our future. The result? Our children see us fretting instead of following a dream. Ask yourself what your vision for your life is—where do you want to be in five, ten, or twenty years? What's the first step you need to take to reach these aims? Write it down. Now that you know what it is, can you take that step today?

Today

I'll show my child that I look forward to the future.

June 22

"It's fun to set goals, reach goals, and reset them."
Bonnie Blair

Once children become preschoolers, you can encourage them to set simple goals. You might say, "Let's see who can run the fastest," and then race your preschooler across the playground. When you let her win, she'll most likely want to do it again, and you can ask her to set a goal of running even faster this time. If your preschooler can throw a ball four feet in front of him, ask him to throw it even harder to see how far it will go. Encourage him to keep practicing as you cheer him on. When you make goal setting fun and manageable for young children, they learn to enjoy facing—and setting—new challenges.

Today
I'll help a young child to be goal-oriented.

June 23

**"A meaningful book grows more meaningful
as it's reread and savored."**
*Joanne Oppenheim, Barbara Brenner,
and Betty Boegehold*

"Again! Again!" is the common cry when young children enjoy a book and want to hear you reread it. When you finish the story for the second time, your children may ask you to start from the beginning once more. This routine can sometimes become tiresome for grown-ups, but it's stimulating for young children, who learn through the repetition of familiar words and images. Nothing turns children on to reading more than the chance to curl up with a favorite adult and savor a beloved book again and again.

Today
I'll willingly reread a story if asked.

June 24

> **"To retain a sense of community,
> people have to have a sense
> that they're affecting their own lives."**
> *Harold DeRienzo*

The South Bronx in New York was known for having vacant buildings and streets lined with trash and rubble. But Harold DeRienzo believed that he had the power to create a good place to live, and he found people on Kelly Street who were willing to help. Together, they cleaned up the streets and planted flowers, gradually transforming the neighborhood for the children and families who lived there. Harold DeRienzo proved that one small idea can create big changes—especially when other people pitch in.

Today

**I'll consider ways to make my neighborhood
a better place.**

June 25

**"Support can happen in schools
in a number of ways:
being noticed, named, included, and encouraged."**
Peter Benson, Ph.D.

The best childcare settings are filled with caregivers
and children who enjoy learning and being together.
As a teacher or caregiver, you don't necessarily
require funding to develop a caring environment
for young children—but you *do* need caring people.
The staff can help see that all children feel wel-
comed and cared for. Be sure to notice, include, and
value every child—this makes children feel important. Be sure to encourage, support, and nurture
every child—this makes children feel empowered.

Today
**I'll focus on what we're doing well
and how we can improve.**

June 26

> "Education is our passport to the future,
> for tomorrow belongs to the people
> who prepare for it today."
>
> *Malcolm X*

Education is about making a child's world bigger. Taking a young child to a museum, a zoo, a botanical garden, or an aquarium encourages learning and broadens the child's view of the world. But you don't always have to take your child somewhere that requires a long ride or an entrance fee—in fact, you can find new places and faces in your own backyard. How about bringing your child to a drive-in restaurant where you eat in the car, or visiting a neighbor who has a butterfly garden? What about listening to stories on tape at the local library or going for a walk in the city? Any new experience can motivate a young child to learn something new.

Today
I'll think of a new place to take my child.

June 27

"The right way is not always the popular and easy way. Standing for right when it is unpopular is a true test of moral character."
Margaret Chase Smith

Young children may not understand the concept of integrity, but they can grasp the idea of "doing the right thing." As children grow, you can encourage them to stand up for their beliefs. For example, your child may be sensitive to how animals should be treated; if he witnesses other children hurting a pet, your child may speak up and say that it's not okay to treat an animal that way. Perhaps your child may befriend someone who often gets teased by others; she may understand that treating all people with kindness is important. Applaud children when you observe them sticking up for their beliefs—they'll feel good about doing what's right.

Today
I'll encourage a child who takes a stand.

June 28

**"Meaningful family traditions
give our hectic lives some predictability
and provide a sense of security and comfort."**
Mary LoVerde

Traditions connect us to the past and give meaning to the present. Lighting a candle for dinner or inviting young children to help make lunch can be simple, positive ways to show you care. Involve your children in choosing and celebrating traditions. How about making birthday cards by hand or lying on the grass to watch the stars on a summer night? Traditions don't have to be expensive or time-consuming to be meaningful.

Today
I'll revive a family tradition or start a new one.

June 29

**"Love stretches your heart
and makes you big inside."**
Margaret Walker

You may have grown up in a family that didn't express much affection. Maybe you're not used to giving a lot of hugs and kisses, or saying the words "I love you." Part of you may feel that love is too risky—that you've been hurt before and it's best not to express too much. But your young children need your love, and you need to give it—not just for them but for *yourself.* When you open your heart to love, you may be surprised at how good you feel inside. You'll build a stronger bond with your children, too.

Today
I'll fully open my heart.

June 30

**"Keeping your child physically safe
is your most basic responsibility—
and a never-ending one."**
American Academy of Pediatrics

According to the American Academy of Pediatrics, adults can prevent most, if not all, of the accident-related injuries that affect young children. Childhood accidents usually involve three factors: (1) the child, (2) an object that causes an injury, and (3) the environment the child is in. Accidents happen quickly and easily, so be sure your home, classroom, or child-care center is safe for children. Seal electrical outlets with childproof covers, install safety gates, keep cleaners and medicines out of children's reach, and post emergency numbers near every phone. Above all, make sure that young children are supervised at all times.

Today
I'll keep safety in mind.

EMPOWERMENT
ASSET #10: SAFETY

July 1

**"As children learn to accept responsibility
they begin to enjoy being responsible."**
Don Dinkmeyer, Ph.D., and Gary McKay, Ph.D.

Some responsibilities may seem overwhelming to
young children. For example, a four-year-old who's
asked to clean his or her messy room may quickly
feel frustrated if there are lots of clothes, toys, shoes,
game pieces, crayons, and balls on the floor. You can
help your child turn this big chore into several
smaller ones and work together to get the job done.
You might begin by sorting the clothes and tossing
them into the hamper (if you turn this into an
impromptu basketball game, you'll both have more
fun). Next, you might pick up the crayons and put
them back in the box. Then take a break: play a
short game, get a snack, or read a story. When you
and your child return to the task, it won't seem so
big anymore.

Today
I'll help my child break a large task into small ones.

July 2

**"What its children become,
that will the community become."**
Suzanne LaFollette

Many communities now have initiatives that focus on infants, toddlers, and preschoolers. For example, in Glenwood Springs, Colorado, parent educators visit the homes of new parents to demonstrate how to care for young children. Kids sell fortune cookies that contain child-friendly messages. Local teenagers have created a coloring book to teach toddlers and preschoolers how to grow up to be caring, productive adults. These efforts have shown how people of *all* ages can help to bring out the best in young children. What might your community do?

Today
I'll identify one way my community can support young children.

EMPOWERMENT
ASSET #7: COMMUNITY VALUES CHILDREN

July 3

"Foster a sense of community among students."
Alfie Kohn

Children are happier in their childcare centers and preschools when they feel a sense of belonging and have a bond with their teachers and caregivers. To help young children feel more secure and loved, you can sit on the floor as you teach, so you're at the same level as the children. During playtime, join in with their games and activities. During storytime, let the children take turns sitting beside you and turning the pages. Like adults who perform better on the job when they feel connected and respected, children learn more easily when they feel they're part of a caring group of people.

Today
I'll help children feel more connected.

July 4

"I like the dreams for the future better than the history of the past."
Thomas Jefferson

Americans celebrate the Fourth of July with picnics and fireworks, but during all the fun, it's easy to forget what this holiday is really about. The Declaration of Independence—signed by fifty-six members of the Continental Congress—marked a break from the British government and declared that the American people had the right to autonomy. In one sense, the document is a symbol of personal power—of individuals standing up for their beliefs, coming together as one, and changing the rules as a result. Whether or not you live in the U.S., you can share the idea of personal power with your young child—and celebrate freedom.

Today

I'll remember what Independence Day is about.

July 5

**"Children not only like to play
with their special friends but like to sit
with arms around each other and whisper."**
Louise Bates Ames, Ph.D.

Four- and five-year-olds are often very affectionate
with their friends. They like to hug and kiss each
other and hold hands, whether they're boys or girls.
You can compliment young friends when they get
along well. You might say, "You and Jamal have lots
of fun together," or "I like how you and Eliza laugh
and play together so well." Don't be surprised,
however, if preschoolers who are the best of friends
suddenly bring each other to tears—they can act
loving one moment and squabble the next. If
needed, step in and help them resolve the conflict.
Afterward, show them that friends can make up
with hugs and go back to being just as close as they
were before.

Today
I'll help children stay friends.

July 6

"We are indeed much more than what we eat, but what we eat can nevertheless help us to be much more than what we are."
Adelle Davis

Many parents struggle with picky eaters—children who like few foods and are reluctant to try anything new (especially if it's green and leafy). If you've got a picky eater at home, you may often tire of the whining and resistance that accompanies most meals. But good nutrition isn't only a positive value—it's an important boundary, too. When you stick to healthy choices, you're sending a message that nutrition counts. You might make a rule that children have to try one bite. If they don't like a food, don't force the issue, but tell them you're glad they tried it. Often, young children's food tastes change without warning: what they don't like one month becomes a favorite the next.

Today
I'll help my child take at least one bite.

July 7

**"The best way to protect a child
is to make sure an adult accompanies her
whenever she crosses a street."**
June Rogoznica

Experts say a child needs to know twenty-six separate skills to cross a street alone. Some of these skills can be taught to young children, while others won't develop until children are older. For example, kids don't use their peripheral vision well until about age eleven; when a ball rolls into the street, young children will stay focused on the ball—not on anything else. To avoid danger, keep a close eye on young children as they play outdoors. Teach them the essential skills of holding an adult's hand, looking both ways before crossing the street, and choosing the best place to cross, such as a crosswalk or an intersection.

Today
I'll help a young child safely cross the street.

July 8

"Concentration is everything."
Luciano Pavarotti

What's one of the most frustrating things that can happen when you're fully involved in an activity? Getting interrupted. When young children are engaged in an activity, you may be tempted to interrupt to show them a better way, offer advice, or comment on how well they're doing. Although you may have good intentions, the result is a break in children's concentration. Being able to focus is an important skill that young children need to develop. You can help by waiting until children finish before offering any comments or suggestions.

Today
I'll give children uninterrupted time to learn.

July 9

**"The battles that count aren't the ones
for gold medals. The struggle within yourself—
the invisible, inevitable battles inside all of us—
that's where it's at."**
Jesse Owens

When we see successful people, we tend to notice
only what they've achieved, not the process they
went through to get where they are. Jesse Owens
was the first American to win four gold medals in
Olympic Track and Field in a single day. But just as
important are the struggles he faced while becoming a champion. As a teen, he was unable to participate in after-school running practices because he
had to work to help his family financially. As a college student, he wasn't allowed to live on campus
because of his race. Despite a back injury, he set
three world records and tied a fourth at the 1935 Big
Ten meet. When you talk to young children about
heroes, help them see that with a strong sense of
purpose, people overcome even the greatest odds.

Today
I'll teach that success takes hard work.

July 10

**"The main source of good discipline
is growing up in a loving family,
being loved, and learning to love in return."**
Benjamin Spock, M.D.

How do you determine the consequences of children's actions or behavior? Educator Barbara Coloroso advises using the acronym RSVP when responding. Think *R* (Is it reasonable?), *S* (Is it simple?), *V* (Is it a valuable learning tool?), *P* (Is it practical?). For example, if a child throws a tantrum in frustration, the solution isn't to yell or punish. It's reasonable, simple, valuable, and practical to let the child cry; once the tears are done and the child is calmer, you can talk about what's bothering him or her. No matter what the behavior, children deserve to be treated in a respectful, loving way. Enforcing family boundaries is about using our heads—and our hearts.

Today
I'll think "RSVP" before reacting.

July 11

"Oh, who are the people in your neighborhood?"
Jeff Moss

This familiar line from a *Sesame Street* song introduces young children to the people who live and work in their communities. You can introduce your young child to the working people he or she meets during the day—the postal carrier, the cashier at the grocery store, the bus driver, the librarian. Help your child meet the neighbors, too. Take him or her for a walk in a stroller or wagon, making a point of talking or waving to the people you meet. Help your child make connections, such as knowing the name of the neighbor who has the friendly dog or the one who has lots of grandchildren.

Today

I'll introduce my child to people in our area.

July 12

**"Young children will approach new relationships
with confidence if they've already had
some positive experience in accepting authority
from adults outside their family."**
Lilian G. Katz, Ph.D.

Part of growing up is learning that the world is
more than what takes place at home. Little by little,
young children discover that their world includes
not only their home but their childcare center or
school, their neighborhood, and their community.
They begin to build relationships with other
adults—teachers, caregivers, neighbors, or members of their faith community. You can encourage
your child to develop these relationships by helping
to build trust. You might say, "Mrs. Garcia wants to
show you her fish tank. You can hold her hand and
look at the fish together while I wait over here." As
your child becomes more comfortable, you can
gradually let him or her spend more time with other
caring adults.

Today
I'll help my child spend time with another adult.

SOCIAL COMPETENCIES
ASSET #33: INTERPERSONAL SKILLS

July 13

**"If you do not tell the truth about yourself,
you cannot tell it about other people."**
Virginia Woolf

Although young children are by nature self-absorbed, they're just beginning to understand themselves in a bigger way. We can help by talking with children about what we observe in them; when we do, we're teaching them to become more observant of and honest with themselves. "That puzzle seems to be frustrating you," or "You seem so happy today!" not only helps young children name what they're feeling but also lets them know that their emotions are okay. And when young children are able to tell you if they feel crabby, angry, or sad, you'll know that they're beginning to look at and express themselves in an honest way.

Today
I'll teach my children to be honest about feelings.

July 14

"The playground exposes toddlers to new challenges and allows them to explore different surfaces and textures than the familiar ones at home."
Desmond Kelly, M.D.

July is National Recreation and Parks Month—an ideal time to take young children to a park or playground to experience the sights, sounds, smells, and textures of the great outdoors. At a playground, toddlers and preschoolers can swing, climb, slide, crawl through tunnels, and explore a world that's very different from the one at home. At a park, they can smell the flowers, touch the trees, watch the bugs and birds, and breathe the fresh air. As you explore the outdoors with young children, you'll probably hear joyful shouts of "Look at me!" and "Look at that!" Children love playing outside and exploring new places—and you will, too.

Today
I'll take a child to a park or playground.

July 15

**"'Now stop!' Max said and sent the wild things
off to bed without their supper."**
Maurice Sendak

When Max, the hero of *Where the Wild Things Are,*
commands the beasts to stop being so wild, he
shows them how powerful he is, even though he's
just a small boy. Like Max, young children seem to
take great satisfaction in saying "Stop" and "No."
This kind of resistance is also a way of saying *yes*. If
children say no to cuddling, they may be saying yes
to needing time alone. If they say no to what's
on their plate, they may be saying yes to needing to
make choices about the foods they eat. When
children resist, notice what they *do* want as well as
what they don't want.

Today
I'll be understanding when children say no.

July 16

"Names are strange and special gifts."
Michael Dorris

Many parents struggle over what to name their child, and throughout pregnancy or the adoption waiting period, they may create long lists of possibilities. Some examine their family trees, while others go to bookstores or libraries to look at the countless baby-name books available. At age three or older, your child may ask, "Why did you name me _____?" You can use this as an opportunity to talk about the history of your child's name. Show your family tree and where the name appears, or get out the baby-name book and read the meaning of the name aloud. Talk about ways that the name suits him or her. If your child is ready, sit down together and practice writing your names.

Today
I'll talk with my child about his or her name.

July 17

**"All children have the capacity
to be both kind and cruel."**
Barbara Unell

We all have days when we don't feel very nice, but young children are especially volatile and prone to acting on their emotions. A child may hug a friend one moment—and slug him the next. By teaching and reinforcing kindness, we can show that learning how to be kind is as important as learning the ABCs and 1-2-3s. Toddlers and preschoolers can learn about kindness as they care for their stuffed animals or dolls. You can also teach them about caring by showing them how to nurture living things: fill a birdfeeder together, water some plants, comb a pet's fur, or visit an animal shelter and volunteer to walk and spend time with a dog. There are many ways to care and be kind.

Today
I'll help my child show kindness.

July 18

**"Most of the people I know who have
what I want—which is to say, purpose, heart,
balance, gratitude, joy—are people with a deep
sense of spirituality."**
Anne Lamott

Religious congregations can be very different from
one another, even if they're the same denomination
or follow the same religious tradition. Some may
emphasize perseverance and humility, while others
focus on values like peace and justice. When you
visit a congregation, you can ask about its over-
arching theme or mission, in addition to the activities and programs that are offered. Once you find
and join a congregation that fits your values and
principles, you'll be introducing your children to an
extended community of people with shared beliefs
and interests.

Today
**I'll learn more about the congregations
in my community.**

July 19

**"Life is just a series
of trying to make up your mind."**
Timothy Fuller

Young children love to talk about their birthdays. Toddlers and preschoolers may ask again and again about the date of their birthday; they may wonder aloud what the weather will be like; they may constantly suggest ideas for a cake, activities, or people to invite. Even though young children may have trouble making up their minds, let them get involved in birthday planning—their own birthdays and those of other family members. Together, decide on who to invite, what kind of cake or ice cream to serve, and what the theme will be. Have fun making simple decorations like paper chains and "Happy Birthday" signs.

Today
I'll let my child help me plan.

July 20

**"Then mooing and baaing and clucking
and quacking, they all set to work on their farm."**
Martin Waddell

In the children's book, *Farmer Duck,* a duck has to do all of the daily chores while the lazy farmer sleeps the day away. The other farm animals feel this is unfair, and they agree to help the duck with his work. This book can help young children see the importance of doing their share, so that the household chores are easier on everyone. You may want to read this book aloud, and then talk about ways that toddlers and preschoolers can pitch in. Ask them about simple ways they can help. Can they put their shoes in the closet after they take them off? Can they throw away their napkins after a snack? To make these tasks more fun, suggest that children moo, baa, cluck, and quack as they do them!

Today
I'll encourage my children to do their part.

July 21

"An aim in life is the only fortune worth finding."
Jacqueline Kennedy Onassis

Finding a sense of purpose is about doing something meaningful, worthwhile, and enjoyable. While young children aren't ready to find an aim in life, they *are* able to find an aim of the day, hour, or moment. What's important is that for a particular day, hour, or moment the child feels purposeful. Discovering new animals at the zoo, coloring a picture, digging holes in the sand, blowing bubbles, or watching ants run in and out of an ant hole are all activities that can give young children a sense of purpose and meaning. What activities might fascinate your child? You can help find them.

Today
I'll find an activity that captures my child's attention.

July 22

"No one rises to low expectations."
Les Brown

It's often quicker and easier to do things for pre-schoolers instead of letting them do things them-selves. We may fix their cereal, dress them, and comb their hair in the rush to get out the door in the morning. But when we do this, we show children that we don't expect much of them. Preschoolers want and need to take care of themselves in small ways. They can pour cereal—though much of it may end up on the table instead of in the bowl. They can put on their clothes—though they may have trouble with buttons and laces. They can comb their hair—though it may still have a few tangles afterward. Be patient and willing to accept imperfection. Over time, young children will master these tasks.

Today
I'll let a child do something on his or her own.

July 23

"Children want the attention of their mother or father more than they want anything else."
Marianne Daniels Garber, Ph.D.

July is National Purposeful Parenting Month. It's a month for parents to reflect on their roles—and then act. Remember, children *want* to be with Mom or Dad, playing, snuggling, laughing, and learning. Although your days may be busy and stressful, find time to give your child some extra attention. Research from the University of Minnesota shows that children who feel loved and supported grow up more curious, get along better with peers, perform better in school, and better cope with difficulties.

Today
I'll give my child extra attention.

July 24

"Caring can create possibilities for children—
possibilities for learning to read,
for recognizing their capabilities and feeling better
about themselves, for learning how to work
and play with others."

G. Noblit, D. Rogers, and B. McCadden

Teachers and caregivers have a powerful role in creating caring out-of-home environments for young children. For example, teachers and caregivers who read aloud, plan activities, encourage exploration, and sit on the floor to play with children create a caring community. On the other hand, if adults take a more passive role and interact with children mainly when mishaps occur, young children won't feel as supported—they may even learn that misbehavior leads to adult attention. Be sure that your classroom or childcare center is a place where young children not only interact with each other but also with the adults who care for them.

Today
I'll interact with children in a caring way.

July 25

"We must start with the ABCs of good health and build on that foundation. This is the way to give our children the knowledge and the skills they need."
Jocelyn Elders, M.D.

Children don't learn about a healthy lifestyle on their own. As adults, it's our job to see that young children eat broccoli or carrots instead of french fries, and that they get outside to run and move instead of sitting in front of the television. Take the time to discuss food and activity choices and the reasons behind them. Young children delight in hearing that eating oranges can help keep illness away, that drinking milk can make bones and teeth healthy, and that exercising builds strong muscles. This knowledge will help them understand the healthy choices you make for them.

Today
I'll explain the healthy choices I make.

July 26

**"When discipline is seen as teaching
and is conveyed with empathy and nurturing,
children feel good when they comply."**
*T. Berry Brazelton, M.D.,
and Stanley I. Greenspan, M.D.*

When we view discipline as *teaching,* we become more patient with children. We correct them in a much more loving, compassionate way. Suppose a toddler or preschooler gets mad and purposely throws food on the floor. You might say, "I see you're done with your meal. Now you can help me clean up this mess." Help the child get down from the table or high chair and wipe up the spilled food with you. As you do this, talk about better ways to express angry feelings. Teachers know that children don't learn in one lesson. Teaching takes years. Learning takes practice.

Today
I'll see discipline as teaching.

July 27

*"The emotions of prejudice are formed
in childhood, while the beliefs
that are used to justify it come later."*
Thomas Pettigrew

You may have some prejudices that you learned as a young child. Even if nothing negative was said, you sensed something was going on if your mom or dad avoided certain parts of town. As a parent, you need to actively work at not passing on prejudices—even ones you may not be fully aware of. Ask yourself if you've unwittingly made negative comments about certain groups of people: men or women; the young or old; people of a different race or religion; democrats or republicans; the wealthy or poor; those who live in cities or in the suburbs. Your children can't help but hear these remarks and form their own conclusions.

Today
I'll be aware of how prejudices affect my children.

July 28

**"As we teach our children how to respond
to the call of charity, we are showing them
that we value their contributions."**
Deborah Spaide

When we provide service projects for children to do,
we empower them. Preschoolers can share books
with infants and toddlers by making up a story to
the pictures or reciting the words from memory; or
they can entertain a baby with a rattle or soft toy.
A toddler or preschooler can get a diaper or a burp
cloth for an adult who needs help with an infant.
Finding meaningful ways for young children to
serve builds their sense of confidence and caring. Be
sure to thank them for each helpful thing they do.

Today
I'll thank a child who helps.

EMPOWERMENT
ASSET #9: SERVICE TO OTHERS

July 29

**"Education should be the process
of helping everyone to discover his uniqueness."**
Leo Buscaglia

As parents, teachers, and caregivers, we often focus on specific learning achievements: new words a baby can say, different colors a toddler can identify, or how well a preschooler can write his or her name. And in our excitement, we may even begin homework and workbooks with young children. Yet, the best kind of learning for young children is more basic: getting to know themselves, asking for what they need, and getting along with other people. Young children who have these skills are more likely to do well in school than children who don't.

Today
I'll focus on the skills my child really needs.

July 30

**"Having a tantrum is really
a primitive form of communication."**
Marilyn Webb

When a young child gets mad at you, you know it.
Young children's anger is often expressed physically
(and noisily)—they yell, scream, stomp their feet,
throw a tantrum, or even fling themselves on the
floor. Children may act this way when they're
frustrated and don't have the words to express their
feelings. But some tantrums have a different purpose: children may use them to gain power or to
force you to give in. What should you do? Ignoring
the tantrum is often best; if possible, leave the room
but keep the child in view. Another option is to use
a time-out. Have the child sit in a chair for a few
minutes until he or she has calmed down. Later
explain, "When you act like that, we need a break
from each other. Let's talk about how you felt."

Today
I'll be patient when a child's upset.

SOCIAL COMPETENCIES
ASSET #36: PEACEFUL CONFLICT RESOLUTION

July 31

"Look for the strengths in every child's behavior."
Jane Nelsen, Ed.D.

Sometimes it's easier to notice what young children do wrong in a neighborhood than what they do right. A toddler may exuberantly pick the neighbor's flowers; a preschooler may energetically throw sand while playing in a sandbox with other children. It's important to remember that young children are still learning the rules, and they often don't realize when they do harm. Gently correct them when needed, but be sure to notice what children are doing *right*, too. Give a compliment to a child who picks up his or her trash, for example. Or affirm a child who wears a helmet while riding a tricycle or bike.

Today
**I'll focus on how children
make my neighborhood more fun.**

August 1

"I try to do the right thing at the right time."
Kareem Abdul Jabbar

You're caught in a traffic jam and your children are fighting in the back seat of the car—you want to yell, but you know this will send them the wrong message. The family cat jumps on the countertop and knocks several dishes on the floor—you're tempted to spank him, but you believe in treating animals with respect (and you know your children are watching to see what you'll do). At times like these, it's easy to yell, curse, or lose your temper—it's not so easy to keep your cool. Your integrity may be tested when you least expect it. You can be ready and do the right thing.

Today
I'll make sure my actions match my beliefs.

August 2

**"Friendship is the only cement
that will ever hold the world together."**
Woodrow Wilson

August 2 is Friendship Day. When Sark was a young girl, her best friend was an eighty-year-old neighbor named Mr. Boggs. He let Sark ride her trike and bike in his driveway. When Mr. Boggs got sick, Sark made him a card or a drawing every day and sent it to the hospital. A month later, he said, "You saved my life. No one else called or wrote. Your mailings gave me the courage to live." You can look for senior citizens that your child can get to know in your neighborhood, extended family, or congregation. Older people enjoy spending time with young children, and children learn a lot about friendship from the way older people smile at them, listen to them, and talk with them.

Today
I'll help my child befriend an older person.

August 3

"The success of each generation of children is contingent on the efforts of caring adults. We must all become supporters and advocates for children."
Senator Nancy Kassebaum

All of the neighborhood children know where Gary and Carrie Surber live. The Surbers, who have a young daughter, have made their home and yard a gathering place for any child who wants to visit. Children play games, run races, or simply come to talk in the Surber's backyard or on their front porch. This simple gesture has turned into a major form of support for young children. You don't have to do a lot to get to know children—you just need to be interested in them and make your home or yard a welcoming place.

Today
I'll welcome young children into my life.

SUPPORT
ASSET #3: OTHER ADULT RELATIONSHIPS

August 4

> "Giving children the feeling of being cared about
> for themselves, not just for their performance,
> is integral to their self-esteem."
> *Richard Oberfield, M.D.*

It's exciting to watch young children grow and learn new things. You may get a feeling of pride when your baby begins to crawl, when your toddler starts to talk, or when your preschooler writes his or her name for the first time. But it's important to love and encourage young children for who they *are*—not just for what they *do*. When you greet your child in the morning or tuck him or her in at night, remember to say "I love you" or "You're special to me." When you go for a walk together in the park, you might say, "I really enjoy being with you." If your child misbehaves, you might say, "I don't like it when you push, but I love you no matter what you do." When children feel loved for who they are, their self-esteem soars.

Today
I'll love my children no matter what they do.

August 5

**"You never learn anything
like you learn it by experiencing it."**
Alice Neel

Experience is a young child's best teacher. Toddlers and preschoolers can learn about their senses when you let them experience different things to touch and smell. Give toddlers various objects to touch: a cup of water, sandpaper, a rubber toy, a feather, a rock. Talk about how each object feels: "Which one is wet?" "Which one is soft?" "How does the sandpaper feel?" Preschoolers may enjoy a game where they have to identify different items by their smell. Start by blindfolding the children; hold each item under their nose and ask them to guess what it is. You might try a flower, some chocolate, clay, spices, and an orange.

Today
I'll create sensory experiences.

August 6

"Bullying is the most common form of violence facing children today."
Johnson Institute

Even young children can be bullies. Bullying can mean hitting, kicking, pushing, biting, or making threats such as, "If you won't play with me, I won't invite you to my birthday party." You can teach toddlers and preschoolers to deal with other young children who use aggression for power or control. You might start by talking about what bullies do: "Bullies use force to get what they want. They may hit or say mean words." Let children know that they have choices for dealing with a bully. They can say, "I don't like what you're doing," they can walk away, and they can tell a parent or teacher what happened. If you see a child acting like a bully, take him or her aside and explain why you won't accept this behavior.

Today
I'll teach children to handle bullying.

August 7

**"Treat your children as individuals
without reinforcing stereotypes."**
Leon Hoffman, M.D.

Many preschools and childcare centers are diverse,
culturally aware places. They may have posters
showing people of many races, dolls of different
ethnicities, crayons of many tints and hues (so
children can create different skin tones), and books
with illustrations and stories that depict various
cultures—all good ways to affirm children's backgrounds. Sometimes what's overlooked, though, is
family diversity. We need to remember that children
live in all kinds of homes: adoptive, interracial, or
single-parent, for example. Some children may live
in a foster home or have gay or lesbian parents. Be
sure that your school or childcare center acknowledges nontraditional homes and helps all children
become aware that diversity extends to families, too.

Today
I'll be conscious of family diversity.

SOCIAL COMPETENCIES
ASSET #34: CULTURAL COMPETENCE

August 8

**"How men think about fatherhood
helps us understand how they think
about themselves as men."**
Robert Griswold

Dads who are involved with their children can have
a huge impact on their lives. One study found that
dads who attended school conferences and child
study groups were more likely to read and tell stories
to their children at home. Fathers who are involved
in their children's activities—at home and away
from home—show their children the vital role that
dads play in children's daily lives. If you're a father,
be involved: get to know your children's care
providers, attend conferences, and read and play
games. If you're a mother, teacher, or caregiver, find
ways to encourage fathers.

Today
**I'll be a supportive dad—
or support the dads I know.**

August 9

"When I was young, my ambition was to be one of the people who made a difference in this world. My hope still is to leave the world a little bit better for my having been here."
Jim Henson

When Jim Henson—the creator of *Sesame Street* and original puppets he dubbed "muppets"—died unexpectedly in 1990, fans around the world deeply mourned the loss of the man who, through his technical and artistic talents, brought smiles to the faces of adults and children alike. Henson was a model for his son, Brian, who today carries on his father's legacy by continuing to create muppets for television and movies. As a parent, you too can be a model for your children, demonstrating how you're motivated to do well at home, at work, in the community, and in the world. Help your children see what motivates you to succeed and make a difference each day.

Today
I'll model motivation for my children.

August 10

"The ultimate in art is self-expression, not escape."
Duke Ellington

Psychologists often encourage young children to share their feelings by drawing pictures or telling stories—children often feel freer to express themselves through art, songs, storytelling, creative movement, or dramatic play. You can encourage children to creatively express their feelings by providing lots of hands-on materials: puppets, paper, crayons, play dough or clay, musical instruments, blocks, dress-up clothes, and sidewalk chalk. Turn on different types of music (children's songs, jazz, classical, country, or rock) as the children play; the sounds will further spark their imaginations.

Today
**I'll help children
to creatively express their emotions.**

August 11

**"The merits of good childcare
for all who need it or want it are many."**
Susan Castro

Each year, *Working Mother* magazine publishes a state-by-state guide that rates childcare settings according to quality. The Children's Defense Fund also ranks childcare by state on its Web site (*www.childrensdefense.org*). You can find out what model states are doing: Rhode Island, for example, created a program to provide health benefits to childcare workers; Oklahoma expanded its pre–K program so that every four-year-old in the state would be eligible to attend. By writing to your legislative representatives and voting for people who have concrete agendas to put children first, you can advocate for higher quality childcare for the children in your state.

Today
I'll learn more about my state's quality of childcare.

August 12

"The one crucial thing that binds a family together is the faith of each member that when he or she has something to say, the others will listen."
Garrison Keillor

That old standby "How was your day?" may not seem like stimulating dinner-table conversation, but it does help open the lines of communication between family members. You might try a variation like, "What was the best thing that happened to you today?" or "What questions did you ask today?" You can make a point of turning off the TV and talking during meals; you can hold regular family meetings to see how each person is doing—even your youngest children will enjoy participating if the meetings are short. When family members talk and listen on a regular basis, everyone feels more connected.

Today
I'll talk to my child about his or her day.

August 13

**"Through the use of books
I had the whole world at my feet:
could travel anywhere, meet anyone,
and do anything."**
Benjamin Carson

Stories have the power to transport children to far-away places—and so do illustrations. Young children who can't yet read enjoy looking at a book's pictures to figure out what the story says or to make up words of their own. You may want to choose picture books that have won the Caldecott Medal—awarded annually by the Association for Library Service to Children (ALSC) to honor the year's most distinguished American picture book for children. Many public libraries have a special section for Caldecott-winning books or a list of the titles that have earned the award throughout the years. You may even want to choose picture books that don't have any words—you and a child can then make up the story yourselves.

Today
I'll share a picture book with a child.

COMMITMENT TO LEARNING
ASSET #25: READING FOR PLEASURE

August 14

"Home is where the heart is."
American proverb

Families today have busy lifestyles and may feel exhausted after long days of work, school, and other activities. It's easy to slip into the habit of "collapsing" when you get home or hurrying around to take care of responsibilities like feeding your children, bathing them, and getting them to bed on time. Is the atmosphere in your home often low energy or high pressure? If so, you may want to focus on making family time more enjoyable and meaningful. Start by incorporating routines that help each family member feel welcome and relaxed: give hugs, sit down and talk, or take a walk to unwind. Involve young children in helping to prepare dinner or set the table, so you can spend more time together after a long day. Have a dependable bedtime ritual that includes a warm bath, a story, and more hugs.

Today

**I'll find one way to make my home
a place with heart.**

August 15

"Sharing is one of the most challenging social skills for all children to learn. The limits are so unclear. Moms and dads don't share their cars with the neighbors, and yet kids are supposed to."

Mary Sheedy Kurcinka

It's true: we don't usually share our cars with our neighbors, or many of our other belongings either. Yet, we expect our children to share all of their toys with friends and neighbors who visit. This is a difficult task for many toddlers and preschoolers, who may be prompted to shout, "That's mine!" when another child reaches for their favorite toys. To avoid conflict, talk about sharing before a friend comes over to play. You might say, "When Terrance is here, he'll want to play with your toys. You can share to show Terrance that you're a friend." If your child is anxious about sharing a favorite toy or doll, invite him or her to put that item away for safekeeping. Let sharing be a positive choice that your child makes.

Today
I'll help children share.

August 16

"In the first months of life, we have to set limits for our children and, yes, for ourselves."
Robert Coles

When you hear "family boundaries," you may think this refers to setting limits for your children. But family boundaries are about *every* family member: adult or child. As you know, caring for a young child is a 24-hour, 7-day-a-week, 365-day-a-year job—one you may not receive much training for (and one you definitely won't get paid for). It's helpful to set some limits, so you can continue to care for yourself while caring for your child. Allow yourself time to rest and relax; ask a friend or family member to help out, so you can have a little time to yourself.

Today
I'll know my limits.

August 17

"Do whatever you do intensely."
Robert Henri

As young children learn a new skill, they become intense and focused. Take the skill of putting on socks: toddlers may first stretch the sock to fit their foot; they may then get the sock on only halfway before beginning to experiment with folding over the cuff. Once they become more adept, they may try to put socks on other things: stuffed animals, dolls — or even the legs of a child-sized chair! When young children learn and explore this way, they need a little breathing room; avoid stepping in to help unless you're asked. Children can learn by trial and error or by figuring out how to do something on their own.

Today
I'll step back when a child is intensely focused.

COMMITMENT TO LEARNING
ASSET #22: CHILDREN ARE ENGAGED IN LEARNING

August 18

"The community must assume responsibility for each child."
Pearl S. Buck

A community initiative in Seattle, Washington, is called "It's About Time for Kids." An initiative in Boulder, Colorado, is known as "Help Kids Succeed." Austin, Minnesota, has "Cherishing Our Children." All of these programs—started by an individual or a small group—are designed to help these communities become more caring and stimulating places for children and their families to live. How does your community show that it values children? How might you get involved in making your community an even more child-friendly place?

Today
I'll consider the meaning of community.

August 19

"When in doubt, tell the truth."
Mark Twain

Telling the truth can be difficult for children. First, they like to steer situations in their favor: they may say, "A giant tore the pages of this book, not me." And second, young children have vivid imaginations and may confuse reality and fantasy. How do you know when to ignore a made-up tale or point out the truth? You can look at the child's motives and what harm the lie does. If a child tells a story about how she can jump as high as the ceiling, she's simply using her imagination. But if she tells a tale about a bad dog that ate her cookie—so she can get a second cookie—she's lying to get what she wants. You might say, "I saw you eat that cookie yourself. I need you to tell the truth."

Today
I'll point out the truth for a young child.

August 20

"Never let the fear of striking out get in your way."
Babe Ruth

Until Hank Aaron came along, Babe Ruth held the all-time record for the most home runs: 714. Yet, he also struck out 1,330 times—almost twice as often as he hit a home run. As young children try to master new skills, they often become frustrated and discouraged. They may give up because they've experienced a setback and are afraid to try again. You can help by being supportive. For example, if your preschooler is learning to ride a bike with training wheels, he or she may have a lot of trouble working the pedals at first. You can push the bike while your child rides, until the connection is made that pushing the pedals is the way to move the tires. The process may take days, or even weeks, but if you both stick with it, your child will learn not only to ride a bike but also to be persistent.

Today
I'll help a child who's about to give up.

August 21

**"Children deserve to feel safe
in their neighborhoods and schools."**
Jesse Jackson

Every child has the right to live in a safe home in a safe neighborhood—and to attend safe childcare centers, preschools, and congregations. We can empower young children to keep themselves safe by teaching them that their bodies belong to them. If someone—whether an adult or another child— tries to touch them in a way that makes them feel uncomfortable, they should say no and tell a parent or teacher right away. Give young children the words to say: "My body belongs to me. You can't touch me that way." You may want to share picture books about good-touch, bad-touch to help children understand.

Today
I'll teach children about good-touch and bad-touch.

EMPOWERMENT
ASSET #10: SAFETY

August 22

**"What do we live for
if not to make life less difficult for each other?"**
George Eliot

Many of us may be more task oriented than people oriented. If you keep lots of to-do lists and feel a sense of satisfaction when you cross off each task, you may want to create a new checklist for yourself today: a "kind-to" list. On it you can write the names of children and adults for whom you'd like to do something special. Start with just two names, if you'd like, and then add the kind act that you plan to do. How about something as simple as tucking an "I love you" note in your spouse's pocket or helping your young child build a sand castle? (P.S. August 22 is Be an Angel Day—a day to do one small act of service for someone else.)

Today
I'll make a "kind-to" list.

August 23

"We must use time creatively, and forever realize that the time is always ripe to do right."
Martin Luther King Jr.

Parents of young children sometimes feel isolated. Days may seem long when you're caring for a baby on your own or trying to entertain a busy toddler. The good news is that time away from home is essential for young children. Out-of-home activities help them build skills and interact positively with others. Check out community classes designed for infants and toddlers, or visit the park to connect with other parents and their children. Your child will enjoy some time spent away from home in the warm weather—and so will you.

Today
I'll get out with my child.

August 24

**"Let's put our minds together and see
what kind of life we can make for our children."**
Sitting Bull

Giving young children useful roles means putting
our heads together to create meaningful ways for
children to contribute at home, in school, or at a
childcare center. For example, a teacher may assign
a different child to be the "line leader" each day; a
caregiver may ask a child for help handing out
snacks or wiping up spills. At home, parents can
encourage young children to put items away after
each use, to choose pajamas at bedtime, and to help
feed the family pet. Be sure these small responsibilities fit each child's abilities.

Today
I'll ask children to be helpers.

August 25

**"Pick battles big enough to matter,
small enough to win."**
Jonathan Kozel

Adults understand the idea of "picking their battles," but young children haven't yet learned this concept. They may fight about *anything* – big or small. For example, preschool-age siblings may argue over whose drawing is "the best" or get into a fight about whose turn it is to go first in a game. You can help them see that they have the power to solve these problems peacefully. They can make a decision to agree or to take a break from each other. You might say, "Both of you worked hard on your pictures. I'm sure you can agree on that." Or "I'm going to let you two decide how to work this out. One of you can let the other go first, or we can put away the game until another day."

Today
I'll help children work it out.

SOCIAL COMPETENCIES
ASSET #32: PLANNING AND DECISION MAKING

August 26

*"I believe that every right implies a responsibility;
every opportunity, an obligation;
every possession, a duty."*
John D. Rockefeller Jr.

Young children can learn responsibility in a number of ways. You teach them to be responsible when you give them shelves, boxes, or containers to store their belongings in; it's easier for children to pick up their stuff when they have a special place to put it. You teach responsibility when you let your children help; they can match the socks as you fold the laundry, or they can show each other how to use safety scissors. One way to encourage social responsibility is to have a policy that for every new toy or game the children receive, they choose an older toy or game to give away to a charity.

Today
I'll find one way to teach responsibility.

August 27

> "Going to a weekend religious service
> is a major family ritual in American life.
> At its best, it connects a family with a special
> community of belief and support."
>
> *William J. Doherty, Ph.D.*

How often should families attend religious services? For those with young children, it's best to make participation a part of your weekly routine. This helps children see that going to a place of worship is an important activity in their lives. Yet, some families attend sporadically or only on major religious holidays. Research has shown that the older the parents, the more likely they are to attend services regularly. While 44 percent of parents in their twenties attend religious services about once a week, 65 percent of parents in their thirties and forties do. How often does your family attend? Have you considered going more often?

Today
**I'll re-examine how often
we attend religious services.**

CONSTRUCTIVE USE OF TIME
ASSET #19: RELIGIOUS COMMUNITY

August 28

*"Find the good. It's all around you.
Find it, showcase it, and you'll start believing in it."*
Jesse Owens

Young children are concrete learners—they learn by doing. So they'll better understand the ideas of equality and social justice if they see it or experience it firsthand, instead of simply hearing about it. You might give your child lightweight canned foods to place in a donation box, while explaining the importance of sharing with people who have less. Or take your child to an animal shelter and talk about how the animals have been hurt or left behind, but are now being cared for until they find new homes. These hands-on experiences will help your child understand ways that we can make our communities better places for the people and animals who live there.

Today
I'll teach my child about justice in a concrete way.

August 29

"Ama a tu projimo como a ti mismo."
"Love your neighbor as yourself."
Southwestern Spanish proverb

What might you do to show your neighbors that you care? If a neighbor is going on a summer vacation, volunteer to take in the mail and newspaper — have your young child do this task with you. Or pick flowers from your garden with your child to make bouquets for your neighbors. If you and your child are taking the family dog on a walk, find out if your neighbor's child can come with you — a simple way to give your neighbor a short break. Together, you and your child can do something small, but significant, to treat your neighbors well.

Today
**I'll bring my child along
when I do something for a neighbor.**

SUPPORT
ASSET #4: CARING NEIGHBORHOOD

August 30

**"To help students become ethical people,
as opposed to people who merely do what they are
told, we cannot merely tell them what to do.
We have to help them figure out—for themselves
and with each other—how one ought to act."**
Alfie Kohn

Some childcare centers and preschools have found helpful ways of teaching young children how to behave. For example, teachers or caregivers might use a specific stuffed animal who only comes out when someone acts up; if a child hits someone, that child holds the stuffed animal during a time-out. After the child calms down, the teacher may ask what happened, what the child's feelings were, and what he or she thinks should happen now. When you give preschool-age children the opportunity to think about what they've done, they can begin to figure out better ways to behave.

Today
**I'll give a child time to think
about how he or she acted.**

August 31

**"The future belongs to those who believe
in the beauty of their dreams."**
Eleanor Roosevelt

As a parent, teacher, or caregiver, you can help young children follow their dreams and passions. If a preschooler loves drawing or painting and imagines being an artist, share in the excitement by getting paints, brushes, paper, crayons, and markers for your home or childcare center. Head to the library together to find colorful picture books and stories about young artists. If a toddler has a passion for animals, go on nature walks, practice making animal sounds, visit a farm, or cut out pictures of animals from magazines to make a collage. Whether a young child's passion is music, puppets, books, blocks, cars, or dolls, encourage this interest as often as you can.

Today
I'll help a child follow his or her interests.

September 1

"No one can figure out your worth but you."
Pearl Bailey

We *are* the only ones who can know our worth—but this depends, in part, on how worthy we've been made to feel. As young children, we gained self-worth and self-esteem when loving adults helped us feel special. Now that we're grown, we can give the gift of self-esteem to the children in our lives. How? By giving them our full attention, playing with them, and hugging and holding them; by telling them how much they mean to us and how lucky we are to know them. As they grow, these children will know their own worth because at least one person in their life has repeatedly told them how special they are.

Today
I'll show a child how much he or she means to me.

September 2

**"The only pressure I'm under
is the pressure I've put on myself."**
Mark Messier

Our society thrives on instant gratification and immediate results. People drive fast, talk fast, and eat fast—or do all three at once! But children, especially when they're very young, need time and space to grow. Some children are slow to walk or talk or get potty trained. We wonder if there's something "wrong" with them—or with us. We may feel pressured to push them. But children learn and grow in their own good time. Patience is the key.

Today
I'll be patient as children master new skills.

September 3

**"When we know something depends
on our behavior solely, when it's up to us
to make a difference, then we are more likely
to step up to the challenge."**
George H. Wood, Ph.D.

Teaching responsibility isn't only about assigning tasks to young children—it's also about noticing when they contribute without being asked. Be aware of when your toddler points out crumbs on the floor or "cleans" the coffee table with a kitchen towel. Notice when your preschooler brings you a bottle for the baby or pours water into the dog's bowl. Affirm young children when they take initiative. Let them know how much you appreciate their efforts and what a big help they've been to you.

Today
I'll thank my child when he or she helps.

September 4

**"The essence of being human
is that one does not seek perfection."**
George Orwell

Even very young children may feel a need to be "perfect." Your preschooler may get upset if he or she buttons a coat wrong, keeps missing the T-ball, or can't write the letter *K*. This budding perfectionism can lead children to grow up expecting way too much of themselves. It's important that young children see that *everyone*—parents, teachers, caregivers, and grandparents—makes mistakes. You can point out your own mistakes, such as losing your temper or forgetting to buy your preschooler's favorite kind of juice. Talk often about how people aren't perfect and how errors are an important part of learning.

Today
I'll teach that mistakes are okay.

September 5

"Effective teachers spend a significant amount of time during the first two weeks of school establishing rules and procedures."
Edward Wynne and Kevin Ryan

As the new school year begins, you may be surprised to see a chaotic preschool or childcare center. But keep in mind that the initial disorder may be the result of young children not knowing or understanding the rules. As children begin to grow more comfortable with classroom expectations, they're likely to settle down and get used to the new routine. Ask your preschooler about the rules he or she follows while away from home: "Are you allowed to run indoors?" "Are there certain items that can only be touched by grown-ups?" "What happens if a child doesn't follow the rules?" Talking regularly about the rules helps reinforce their importance.

Today
I'll help children learn the rules.

September 6

"All kids are our kids."
Peter Benson, Ph.D.

Although you'll spend a lot more time and energy with the children in your family or in your care, you can influence the lives of children everywhere. Consider the children you have contact with in your neighborhood or in your child's school or childcare center. When you get to know their names, greet them each time you see them, and find little ways to show you care, you give these children the advantage of having other caring adults in their lives. You can also influence children you may never meet: donate time or money to charities that support children, or make children's issues a priority when you vote.

Today
I'll positively influence a child I don't know well.

September 7

> **"By caring for their baby's physical needs, parents are making him feel safe within his own body. But their role goes further: They are also helping him learn to trust his environment, which helps the baby feel safe emotionally."**
>
> *James M. Herzog, M.D.*

Feeding, burping, or changing a crying infant meets the baby's physical needs; holding or soothing an infant helps meet his or her emotional needs. These caring actions build a sense of trust and security — the infant learns that the world is a safe, welcoming place. As they grow, babies also begin to trust in themselves. They find that they can comfort themselves with a thumb, or self-soothe with a soft blanket or toy. September is Baby Safety Month, a time to contemplate our roles as parents and caregivers, and to focus on helping the infants we care for feel more safe and secure.

Today

I'll help an infant feel safe.

September 8

"Fighting is a game where everybody is the loser."
Zora Neale Hurston

It's not unusual for young children to fight to stand up for themselves or their possessions. If someone takes their toy, they may kick or hit to get it back. If another child bumps into them, they may push or yell. These reactions are normal and common. Still, young children can learn that fighting doesn't help. Encourage empathy by teaching children to consider how the other person feels. You might say, "Alberto was wrong to take your truck, but look how he feels now. He's crying because you kicked him." Or "Maya bumped into you by accident. When you yelled at her, she felt sad." Help children figure out a better solution, such as asking an adult for help.

Today
I'll teach young children that fighting never helps.

SOCIAL COMPETENCIES
ASSET #36: PEACEFUL CONFLICT RESOLUTION

September 9

"Ask. Ask. Ask."
Sarah Ban Breathnach

For the most part, parents set the schedules for young children. You decide what day to go to the park, invite a playmate over, or have quiet activities. As long as your child seems content to go along with these plans, you can keep making them. But when your child becomes more verbal, it's important to ask questions about his or her wishes and needs. Start with simple yes or no questions: "Do you want to play in the sandbox now?" Or "Should we invite Emily over?" Once your child learns to talk, you might ask, "What do you want to do today?" You'll help improve your child's verbal skills *and* encourage a sense of independence.

Today
I'll ask what my child wants to do.

September 10

**"I always prefer to believe the best of everybody—
it saves so much trouble."**
Rudyard Kipling

If young children act in inappropriate ways, believe the best of them—give them the benefit of the doubt. For example, a child who hits, punches, screams, or throws things isn't necessarily a "troublemaker"; more likely, he or she needs help expressing feelings. In your home, school, or child-care center, encourage toddlers and preschoolers with the phrase "Use your words." This phrase is simple and effective; when gently repeated, it helps young children understand that they can find words to express "I need help" or "I feel hurt." Soon enough, you may even hear children using the phrase with each other!

Today
I'll tell a child, "Use your words."

September 11

**"We don't have to hunt for our spirituality.
It's a by-product of living our lives."**
Anne Wilson Schaef

Whether or not you attend religious services, you
have beliefs and morals that you live by and share
with your children. Perhaps your children know
that put-downs aren't okay in your home or that
service to others is an important part of your family's life. Even if there's a belief structure in place,
children are likely to ask questions about religion,
starting around preschool age. If you're not sure
about your spiritual beliefs, such questions can be
unsettling. Consider taking some time to think
about what and how you want to teach your
children about religion, so you're prepared when
questions arise. You may want to seek the advice
of relatives, friends, or even a religious advisor.

Today
**I'll consider what my children need to know
about spirituality.**

September 12

"Cuando una puerta se cierra, cien se abren."
"When one door closes, a hundred open."
Southwestern Spanish proverb

As adults, it's common to feel stuck when our responsibilities (parenting, work, finances, family commitments) seem to limit our choices. If you feel this way sometimes, try to look at your life from a more positive perspective. For example, maybe being a parent has temporarily limited your career choices or affected your budget—but what have you *gained?* For starters, you're facing one of the most rewarding and fulfilling challenges that life can offer. Doors aren't closing—they're opening all around you.

Today
I'll get some perspective.

POSITIVE IDENTITY
ASSET #40: POSITIVE VIEW OF PERSONAL FUTURE

September 13

"When we were just three and four years old, we would make weekly visits to the library, and my mother would say, 'Do you see all these books? Once you're able to write your name, all of these books will be yours.'"
Gloria Naylor

Writer Gloria Naylor first realized the power of the written word when she learned to write her name, obtained a library card, and discovered the world of books that lay at her fingertips. Taking a child to the local library is one of the best routines that an adult can start—it encourages a love of reading and the written word. In the U.S., September is Library Card Sign-Up Month, so take your young child to get his or her own library card. While you're there, check to see if the library has regular story hours where librarians read aloud to a group.

Today
I'll help my child get a library card.

September 14

"There's no such thing as other people's children."
Hillary Rodham Clinton

Sometimes it can be easy to overlook or ignore children who aren't your own. Maybe they're playing so well at the playground that you hardly notice they're there. Or maybe they're arguing over the swings, but you assume their parents will deal with it. Instead of viewing these children as other people's kids, try envisioning them as yours. When you see children playing well, compliment them the way you would your own. When it appears they may be misbehaving, give them gentle guidance or simply check in to make sure everything's okay. Invite your neighbors to do the same with your child. The children in your neighborhood will feel both appreciated and safe.

Today
I'll feel responsible for neighborhood children.

September 15

"A fertile imagination is the jumping-off point."
Justine Rendal

Young children often can stay busy with activities, but at times, they need a creative spark. Suppose your preschoolers are playing in the sandbox, and their interest begins to wane. You might ask questions or suggest alternatives to stir their imaginations: "What if you had some water to pour on the sand?" "What else can you do with the buckets and shovels?" "How about digging a big hole?" "Is there any buried treasure to find?" Thoughtful questions can help renew children's interest, encourage them to experiment, and spur questions of their own.

Today
I'll ask questions to keep children's interest.

September 16

> **"Parents are one available but untapped
> and undirected resource that teachers
> can mobilize to help more children master
> and maintain needed skills."**
>
> *Joyce Epstein*

Need help? More resources? Extra supplies or volunteers? If your school or childcare center needs anything, why not tap in to one of the most reliable sources: parents. Often, parents want to help but aren't sure what to do. As a teacher or caregiver, you can feel free to speak up about what you and the children may need. One childcare center wanted to create a safer playground and asked parent volunteers to help lay some wood chips. One preschool needed walls painted and got parents to sign up for the job. You might see if parents can read during storytime, demonstrate a skill, or talk to your group about their family's customs and traditions. Many parents want to be more involved—all you've got to do is ask.

Today
I'll use parents as a resource.

September 17

"Children need to know and have the right to know the names for body parts. Children gain confidence from knowing the real words."
Anne C. Bernstein, Ph.D.

As young children grow, they're discovering their bodies. Toddlers and preschoolers begin noticing and talking about the differences between the bodies of boys and girls. Some parents are tempted to make up nicknames for private body parts, but it's important to teach young children the correct names to avoid confusion later. Being straightforward helps young children understand that you're comfortable talking about the human body and sexuality.

Today
I'll help my child learn a body part's correct name.

September 18

"Not minding, that's what friends are for."
***Ernie, from* Sesame Street**

On *Sesame Street,* Ernie and Bert are friends—despite their opposite personalities. Ernie is messy, goofy, and mischievous; Bert is neat, serious, and a bit stiff. Somehow, they get past these differences, and even when they squabble, they remember what they like about each other. This unlikely pair helps young children see that people can like different things and act in different ways—yet still be friends. You might encourage children to make friends of a different gender, age, or background. Like Ernie and Bert, children can learn to put aside their differences and find out what friends are for.

Today
I'll teach that friends don't have to be the same.

BOUNDARIES AND EXPECTATIONS
ASSET #15: POSITIVE PEER INTERACTION AND INFLUENCE

September 19

"Our children need tender loving care at every stage of their development."
José Serrano

Some experts refer to toddlers as the "teenagers" of early childhood. Toddlers have a need to be both dependent and independent. They're full of energy; they yell "No!" and "Stop it!"; they want to do things and get frustrated when they can't. If you try to cuddle a toddler, he or she may jump off your lap and find something else to do. If you kiss a toddler, he or she may quickly wipe it off. Yet, toddlers still need support and reassurance from parents. You may find it helpful to ask your toddler before sharing affection: "Can I hug you?" "Do you want a kiss?" "Will you sit on my lap?" And when toddlers *do* ask for affection, give it freely.

Today
I'll show my child love at each age and stage.

September 20

**"This country will not be a good place
for any of us to live in unless we make it
a good place for all of us to live in."**
Theodore Roosevelt

In the U.S., September 20 is Equal Rights Day—a day that celebrates the anniversary of the founding of the Equal Rights Party, which nominated a female presidential candidate in 1884. While the United States has not yet elected a female president, more and more women and people of color are serving in leadership positions. To uphold these role models who are paving new paths, show your preschooler who they are (using magazines, books, or newspapers) and explain what they do. It's important that young children see that regardless of gender, race, or ethnicity, people can lead and make a difference in the world.

Today
I'll show my children all kinds of leaders.

September 21

**"Decide that you want it
more than you are afraid of it."**
Bill Cosby

Young children may fear trying new things, just as adults do. Your preschooler may hang back while other children go on the slide or play a game of Red Light, Green Light. You may be surprised to see your usually talkative child act shy in a group or refuse to participate. If your child seems reluctant—yet you can see that he or she really wants to join in—be encouraging. Help your child focus on the activity, not the fear. You might say, "That slide sure looks like fun. I can watch you climb up and wait for you to come down." Or "Would you like me to introduce you to the other children? They could become your friends." By teaching young children to look past their fears, you give them back some of their personal power.

Today
I'll help a child get past a fear.

September 22

**"A new baby is like the beginning of all things—
wonder, hope, a dream of possibilities."**

Eda J. Le Shan

When a baby is born or an adoptive child arrives, people feel excitement and hope, they bring good wishes and gifts, and they offer their full support. The new child quickly becomes the center of attention, and the parents put most of their energy into arranging family life around him or her. As the months go by, the responsibilities that new parents have don't decrease—but the support they get sometimes does. If you're a friend or relative of new parents, continue to help by baby-sitting occasionally so the parents can go out or finish a few household chores. This is a great way to support the baby, while giving him or her a chance to connect with another adult.

Today
I'll offer to baby-sit.

EMPOWERMENT
ASSET #8: CHILDREN ARE GIVEN USEFUL ROLES

September 23

**"I know her experience with me
has made her into a wonderful, caring person."**
Crista Adamson

Three-year-old Kelsey Adamson knows that her
mom can't give her a bath or fix her hair. Her mom,
Crista, is paralyzed from the neck down. But
Kelsey's mom can read to her before her nap and
take care of her in other ways. And Kelsey knows
that she can help take care of her mom. When she
and her mother go grocery shopping, for example,
Kelsey runs to get the items on their list. Crista has
seen how the family's experience is helping her
daughter to be caring and to look out for those in
need. *All* families face challenges—large and small.
When we face these challenges together with love
and a positive attitude, they not only can bring us
closer but also can make us stronger.

Today
I'll do what I can for my family.

September 24

"A good class helps kids think about their bodies in different ways and presents a focused, problem-solving approach as well as the experience of using their imaginations."
Roberta Altman

Young children are just beginning to see new ways their bodies can move. Two-year-olds enjoy climbing and exploring. Three- and four-year-olds like to jump, hop, gallop, and skip. If you're looking for programs that help young children develop these large-motor skills, consider classes that encourage them to move in creative ways, such as tumbling or creative movement. You can find these classes through your community center, YMCA/YWCA, or local paper, or by asking other parents about programs they've enrolled their children in.

Today
I'll look into movement classes for young children.

September 25

**"Don't neglect the opportunity
to say hello to neighbors."**
Stephanie Mann

The fourth Sunday in September is National Good Neighbor Day. Don't forget that neighbors aren't just the *adults* who live around you but their *children,* too. Take time to notice these young neighbors, learn their names, and find out what they like to do. If they're playing outside, observe them and ask if you can join in. Playing with children—even for just a few minutes—will help you to build a relationship that you can expand on throughout the year.

Today
I'll spend some time with a young neighbor.

September 26

"I prefer to be true to myself."
Frederick Douglass

Young children are good at being true to themselves. Toddlers will play dress-up or play with cars, without regard to gender expectations. Preschoolers will let you know when they need a hug or want to be held. You can help your children stay true to themselves by creating a home environment that values who they are. For example, you can encourage your daughter whether she likes dolls or dump trucks; you can let your son dress up in hard hats and boots or jewelry and fancy shoes. Don't tell young children to "act their age" when they're crying or upset. This message is confusing and can lead children to fear expressing their emotions.

Today
I'll let my children be who they are.

POSITIVE VALUES
ASSET #28: FAMILY VALUES INTEGRITY

September 27

**"Why, sometimes I've believed as many
as six impossible things before breakfast."**
Lewis Carroll

Young children have big imaginations. They imagine
they're tigers, monsters, or clowns. They pretend
to be astronauts, superheroes, or kings and queens.
As they act out these roles, they wonder, experiment,
and create. They stretch their minds and envision
what's possible—even if it's the impossible. Imaginative play helps young children to build a sense of
purpose while making sense of the world. As children play act, ask them what they like about being an
animal or a superhero. "Do you like to fly?" "Do you
enjoy running fast?" "Do you like helping others?"

Today
I'll encourage imaginative play.

September 28

**"To help a child build a healthy, joyful life
is one of the best contributions we can make
toward peace and security in this world."**
Aung San Suu Kyi

Researchers agree that at least one caring adult can
make a difference in the life of a child. All children
deserve to have at least one supportive adult—
besides a caring parent—in their life. Could you be
that adult? Perhaps you can arrange to spend more
time with a young niece or nephew, get to know
a neighborhood child better, or volunteer at a childcare center in your area. Becoming a role model is
a gift that you give to the child, to yourself, and to
the world.

Today
I'll help guide a child.

September 29

**"To argue means to resist,
to say no to another person."**
Carolyn Shantz, Ph.D.

When young children resist, fight, kick, shout, or argue, they're trying to tell you something. Before you can tend to their needs or teach them how to express themselves appropriately, you have to understand what they're communicating. An infant who wants to be left alone may squirm or fuss. A toddler who feels left out may express it by hiding. A preschooler who's afraid may start chasing a pet. It's easy to misinterpret what these children are really trying to say. When you learn to recognize the feelings behind the resistant behavior, you can better address the child's needs.

Today
I'll find out the "why" behind a child's behavior.

September 30

"A mind is a terrible thing to waste."
United Negro College Fund

Children learn by asking questions—often many, *many* questions. As soon as they learn how to talk, they'll often point and ask, "What's that?" Once they have a handle on the names of things, they'll start asking, "Why?" And as their vocabulary increases, so do the questions—and so might your lack of patience. When you spend a lot of time with a young child, these never-ending questions can begin to drive you nuts—but they're a sign of your child's growing curiosity. Take a deep breath, grit your teeth, or smile—and then answer.

Today
I'll answer every question a child asks.

October 1

"Every small item becomes something fascinating."
Vicki Lansky

When babies come across an object they've never seen before, what's the first thing they do? Usually, they grab it and put it in their mouth. Babies do this automatically, as a way to experience and explore something new. You can give a baby creative—yet safe—objects to touch, hold, shake, throw, or roll. He or she may already enjoy rattles, soft toys, and teething rings. You might also let the baby make noise with a set of metal measuring spoons, squeeze a clean sponge (if the baby has teeth, make sure he or she doesn't take a bite), or play Peekaboo under a hand towel. Even simple household objects can become learning tools for a baby.

Today
I'll give a baby something to explore.

October 2

**"Even if it's a little thing, do something
for those who have need of help,
something for which you get no pay
but the privilege of doing it."**
Albert Schweitzer

The idea of serving with a young child can seem overwhelming. Perhaps you'd like to help at a shelter for women who have been abused, but you worry that you'd spend more time looking after your child than actually helping. Teaching your child about volunteering and serving others isn't only about big projects and big issues. Young children can choose an old toy to donate, help plant bulbs for a grandparent or an elderly neighbor, or pick up an empty bottle that someone threw on the ground. Feel empowered to start small.

Today
I'll find a small way for a child to help others.

EMPOWERMENT
ASSET #9: SERVICE TO OTHERS

October 3

"Teach children to be honest with themselves."
Barbara Unell and Jerry Wyckoff

Toddlers sometimes have trouble distinguishing between what's honest and dishonest. A toddler will say a sibling left the toys all over the floor—even if that sibling's at school. A toddler will deny eating the forbidden candy—even though the tell-tale signs are all over his or her face and hands. Don't panic: you aren't raising a liar. This *is* a normal stage of development. You can calmly point out the truth and let your toddler know that fibbing doesn't fool you. When you help young children learn to be honest with themselves, they'll learn to be honest with others.

Today
I'll help children be honest with themselves.

October 4

**"We the people of the United States,
in order to form a more perfect Union,
establish justice. . . ."**
Preamble to the U.S. Constitution

Justice is a tough concept to teach—especially to young children. What you *can* help them learn is that their actions positively or negatively affect others. If a toddler bites another child, you can explain that it's not okay to do so because we need to treat people with care and respect. If a preschooler shares a toy with another child, you can affirm that it's good to think about others. In these ways, you're showing young children the difference between right and wrong. You're allowing them to see that how they act can hurt—or *help*—others.

Today
I'll teach my children that their actions affect others.

POSITIVE VALUES
ASSET #27: FAMILY VALUES EQUALITY AND SOCIAL JUSTICE

October 5

"Give me a laundry list and I'll set it to music."
Gioacchino Antonio Rossini

Children love to be sung to. They never seem to tire of repetitive songs like "The Wheels on the Bus" or "The Farmer in the Dell." You may find yourself playing recordings of these songs over and over, or singing them yourself. To vary the repertoire, make up your own songs about everyday life with your child. Create songs that describe your child's activities, pets, or siblings. Sing about the weather, bedtime, or taking a bath. And give it a shot—sing about the laundry. Your child will enjoy the familiar sound of your voice, no matter what you sing.

Today
I'll sing about anything.

October 6

"My father didn't do drugs or drink, and he wouldn't let anyone smoke in his house. Those are rules I adopted, too."

Earvin "Magic" Johnson

As a parent, you most likely have rules you've set for yourself at home. Maybe you don't smoke in front of your children, or maybe you limit the amount of television you watch when they're around. Perhaps you're divorced, and you've made a promise to yourself never to speak ill of your former spouse when your children are present. When you have rules like these and stick to them, you're setting an example—and standards—for your children. They grow up knowing what's okay and what's not okay in your home. If you currently don't have a set of rules you follow or if you aren't consistent with them, think about what your children may be learning. Consider following one rule you're comfortable with, starting today.

Today

I'll think about our family rules.

BOUNDARIES AND EXPECTATIONS
ASSET #11: FAMILY BOUNDARIES

October 7

"Nothing is impossible,
we just don't know how to do it yet."

L. L. Larison Cudmore

As young children begin to understand their personal power, they also begin to understand their lack of it. They discover that certain places are off limits, they're unable to participate in games or activities designed for older children, and they don't yet have the physical skills or size needed to accomplish some of the tasks they want to do. Realizing their limits often frustrates young children. You can help them cope by pointing out what they *can* control, choose, and do. You might say, "When you're older you can play Monopoly, but for now, let's try Chutes and Ladders." Or "I know it's hard to open this umbrella. I'd be glad to help you."

Today
I'll empower a child.

October 8

**"Without heroes, we are all plain people,
and don't know how far we can go."**
Bernard Malamud

Many so-called "unsung" heroes may have an influence on your child, dedicating their time, energy, or money in ways you might not even be aware of. Perhaps a senior citizen reads at your childcare center; maybe a college student shows science experiments to your child's class once a month. Perhaps your child's caregiver uses his or her own money to buy supplies or often works late to plan new and creative lessons. Caregivers of all types—teachers, aides, volunteers, and *you*—help young children see how far they can go in life. You can help your child understand how heroic this is.

Today
I'll celebrate an unsung hero.

BOUNDARIES AND EXPECTATIONS
ASSET #14: ADULT ROLE MODELS

October 9

"Time works wonders."
Hebrew proverb

You've probably heard of "quality time," but there's also something to be said about "quantity time." When you feel pressured to make every minute with your child creative, productive, and educational, you can quickly burn out. So relax. Enjoy spending lots of time with your young child—as much time as you possibly can. You'll find that those "quality" moments slip in (sometimes by accident, sometimes by design). And while these times will make great memories, so will the fact that you were there.

Today
I'll spend "quantity time" with my child.

October 10

**"People in communities, all else equal,
who know their neighbors,
are people who are less fearful."**
Rick Rosenfeld

Many neighborhoods have found that monthly or yearly meetings can be an effective way to get to know people, share news, and talk about issues that affect the community. Often, safety is a major concern or topic of discussion. You may want to initiate one of these meetings yourself and invite a police officer to visit. He or she can talk about the importance of looking out for each other and other ways to stay safe. Young children who attend the meeting may be in awe of or even frightened by an officer in uniform. Talk with the children about how police officers are there to protect people and can be of help whenever someone is in trouble.

Today
I'll meet with my neighbors to discuss safety.

October 11

"To me, nothing can be more important
than giving children books."
Fran Lebowitz

October is National Book Fair Month, a time to celebrate the buying of books. While libraries are invaluable, it's also important for children to have the chance to *own* books. You can buy them used or new, receive some as hand-me-downs, or request them as gifts for your child. However they arrive, books are a priceless source of information and learning. A child who owns books can return to them again and again.

Today
I'll give a book to a child.

October 12

"Preschoolers tend to fight over possessions and issues of space because they see these things—*my* truck, *my* room—as extensions of themselves."
Carolyn Shantz, Ph.D.

Many of the conflicts between toddlers or preschoolers revolve around *things*. But when children fight over toys, they're really fighting about feeling personally invaded. Knowing that children see their toys as extensions of themselves can help us when we mediate these conflicts. We can discuss ownership as well as sharing: "I know that the dinosaur belongs to you, but you're not playing with it so how about letting Misha use it?" Or "I know you want to play with Patrick's doll, but he's using it right now. Is there something you could trade with him?"

Today
I'll mediate if children argue over toys.

October 13

"For adult education, nothing beats children."
Mark Ortman

In our eagerness to teach our children, we may overlook what they're teaching us: compassion, negotiation, fortitude, scheduling, organization, conflict resolution, and time management. They show us how to let loose, be spontaneous, rest when we need to, and become best friends with someone we were mad at minutes ago. They help us remember what it's like to be a child—and they help us to be better adults. Next time you learn a lesson from a preschooler or another young child, thank him or her. You might say, "Thank you for reminding me that yelling doesn't help. Adults sometimes forget." Your kind words will help that child feel special.

Today
I'll learn from the children I care for.

October 14

"There will always be some curve balls in your life. Teach your children to thrive in that adversity."
Jeanne Moutoussasmy-Ashe

Life is full of curve balls. Maybe a grandparent dies, a favorite aunt or uncle moves away, or parents decide to divorce. Unfortunately, we can't completely insulate young children from difficult times. As adults, we have a responsibility to remain calm and reassure children that the world won't end, despite the changes that will occur. It's best to honestly tell a preschool-age child about what's happening (such as Mom and Dad are going to live apart or Grandpa is very sick), instead of hiding the truth. Experts at the Gesell Institute of Human Development further recommend that adults reassure a child that he or she didn't do anything wrong and is still very much loved.

Today
If needed, I'll gently break hard news to my child.

October 15

"There is nothing on this earth more to be prized than true friendship."
Saint Thomas Aquinas

You never know when one of your own friends will become a close friend to your young child. Maybe a favorite coworker will ask to spend time with your child and begin hanging up your child's drawings in her office. Maybe a neighbor will invite your child to go for walks around the block with him. Maybe your best friend will call up and ask to speak to your child—instead of you! Wonderful friendships can develop when adults and children get to know each other better. Encourage these relationships to help your child grow.

Today
I'll help my friend and child to connect.

October 16

**"Students with high hope
set themselves higher goals
and know how to work hard to attain them."**

C. R. Snyder

When researcher C. R. Snyder compared students with equivalent I.Q.s but different academic achievement levels, he found that the difference between them was hope. That is, the high achievers had a lot more hope—or faith in themselves and the future—than the lower achievers did. Even young children can have a positive or negative attitude. Some say "I can't do it" and won't try something because they're afraid to make a mistake. We can teach children to look at themselves and life in a hopeful way. You might reinforce messages like, "We all make mistakes and that's okay," or "You're having a bad day. Let's try to turn it around."

Today
I'll teach hope.

POSITIVE IDENTITY
ASSET #40: POSITIVE VIEW OF PERSONAL FUTURE

October 17

**"You can bring a horse to water,
but you can't make him drink."**
Anonymous

It happens: You plan fun activities for a young child—a visit to the pumpkin patch or a leisurely walk on a fall day—imagining the child's excitement and delight as you choose a pumpkin or pick up fallen leaves to take home. Then your child clings to you and refuses to take part, and you don't know who's more disappointed. Sometimes it's best to just abandon your plans and head home. But at other times, you can act in certain ways to help your child adjust to a new environment or activity. For example, you could interact with the people and scenery around you to show your child how fun—and safe—everything is. When all else fails, save the activity for a new day and give it another try.

Today
I'll understand if things don't go as planned.

October 18

**"No child is ever spoiled by too much attention.
It is the lack of attention that spoils."**

Bessie Blake

Not too long ago, it was generally believed that children could be spoiled by too much attention. But today, child-development experts say this simply isn't so. Newborns and infants should have their needs met as soon as they cry out. Toddlers and preschoolers must be able to depend on us to comfort them, listen to them, and spend time with them. All young children need our attention — let's be generous with it.

Today

I'll give my children attention.

October 19

**"Knowing what you want
is the first step toward getting it."**
Mae West

If knowing what you want is the first step toward getting it, the second step must be asking for help—as any young child well knows. Babies who are determined to get attention will sometimes cry until they do. Toddlers or preschoolers who are set on putting together a puzzle may whine or shout in frustration until an adult comes over to help. Crying, whining, yelling, or fretting are signals that a child needs you. Because young children often don't have the words to express, "Please help me reach this goal," it's up to adults to notice what young children want and help them get it.

Today
I'll pay attention to a young child's goals.

October 20

"Extracurricular activities help children discover who they are and what they like to do."
Diana Townsend-Butterworth

Extracurricular activities for young children don't have to be ongoing or expensive. They can be one-time, one-hour classes or short events and field trips. Petting zoos, free concerts in the park, nature centers, play-and-discover classes, parades, and hayrides all provide new experiences for young children. When you vary your child's activities, you'll discover which ones he or she prefers—sometimes they'll be things you never would have expected! Once you know what your child likes best, you can find ways to explore those activities together in more depth.

Today
I'll make a list of things for us to do.

October 21

> "Childhood is a time of taking in, of observing and imitating, of listening to our parents, our teachers, our peers. From all these sources we internalize various beliefs and attitudes."
> *Patricia O'Gorman, Ph.D.*

Infants learn about the world based on what they see, hear, taste, and touch. But as children grow, they become more tuned in to how others feel. Toddlers and preschoolers can pick up on the moods of the people around them; for example, they begin to sense when an adult is angry or upset. Little by little, children observe and internalize the feelings, beliefs, attitudes, and values that the adults around them project. Be aware of what you're teaching your children through what you say and what you don't say. They're listening and learning from you.

Today
I'll model positive values and beliefs.

October 22

"Don't wait for the teacher to make the first contact; take the initiative yourself."

C. Drew Edwards, Ph.D.

As a parent, you have the power to take initiative. Don't wait for a teacher or caregiver to make the first move—instead, express what's on your mind. If you'd like to have a conference to discuss your child's progress, ask for one. If you're concerned about something your child is saying or doing, talk with the caregiver or teacher to get his or her feedback and perspective. Parent involvement is more than reacting to what preschools and childcare centers offer—it's taking an active role.

Today
I'll let my child's caregiver know what I need.

October 23

"Let children know we are glad they were born."
Jean Illsley Clarke

Children need to hear that you're glad they're here. In fact, they can't hear it enough. When you tell children how much you appreciate or adore them, you build their self-esteem. Take time to tell your toddler or preschooler about the day he or she was born or adopted. Let your child know how excited and happy you felt. You might even want to pull out the photographs of that special day and talk about the moments you remember most. Your child may love the story so much that he or she will ask you to tell it again and again and again.

Today
I'll tell my children how glad I am to know them.

October 24

**"Play is work for [children]
that constantly extends their limits—
it is a most vital creative function."**
Susan Castro

Young children love to pretend to be adults. They may play "house," "school," or "restaurant"; they may act like miniature doctors, cashiers, performers, athletes, veterinarians, or construction workers. You can enhance playtime by offering children different props and equipment, such as child-sized dinnerware and plastic food, a medical kit, a small basketball hoop, plastic tools, and baby cribs. But not all of these materials need to come from a toy store—you can hunt for items at garage sales or stores that sell used goods, or offer children household materials like a measuring tape, plastic cups and spoons, or an old, disconnected telephone.

Today
I'll enhance children's dramatic play.

COMMITMENT TO LEARNING
ASSET #23: STIMULATING ACTIVITY AND HOMEWORK

October 25

"No matter what accomplishments you make, somebody helps you."
Althea Gibson

No one goes through life completely alone. No matter who you are, you've got someone who has supported you in some way. The opposite is true, too: you support others, and this helps you build connections. Today, think about the people in your life who are helpful and supportive. Do you ever (or often) take them for granted? What about your children—who supports them, besides you? Have you thanked any of these people lately? Showing appreciation can be as simple as a phone call or short note—or as elaborate as a handmade card or gift.

Today
I'll thank those who support my child and me.

October 26

**"Life's piano can only produce
the melodies of brotherhood when it is recognized
that the black keys are as basic, necessary,
and beautiful as the white keys."**
Martin Luther King Jr.

Like the keys of a piano, all people—regardless of
skin color—are basic, necessary, and beautiful. This
concept is one that even young children can begin to
grasp, but teaching it needs to be purposeful. While
you might not make racist statements in front of
your child (or ever), do you make statements that
are *complimentary* about people of other races? Have
you commented, for example, on the beauty of an
Hispanic actress, the talent of an African-American
scientist, the sensitivity of a Caucasian teacher, or
the creativity of an Asian artist? By expressing these
beliefs often, you help instill the ideals of equality in
your child.

Today
I'll teach that people of all colors are valuable.

SOCIAL COMPETENCIES
ASSET #34: CULTURAL COMPETENCE

October 27

"The best way to protect your child's teeth is to teach her good dental habits."
American Academy of Pediatrics

October is National Dental Hygiene Month. This is an ideal time to make sure that young children are on their way to developing good dental habits. By age two, children need to have their teeth brushed at least once a day. Most young children swallow toothpaste as you brush, so it's best to use only water or a small amount of a toothpaste that's recommended for young children. By the time children have all twenty of their baby teeth (somewhere between ages two and three), it's time to take the first trip to the dentist. Unfortunately, almost 60 percent of children have cavities by age three. Your dentist will have tips on preventing them.

Today
I'll remember the importance of dental hygiene.

October 28

**"Kind words can be short and easy to speak,
but their echoes are truly endless."**

Mother Teresa

Kind words and unexpected praise can speak volumes. When was the last time you complimented your child or thanked him or her for being part of your life? You might say, "I sure am lucky to have you," or "I love the way you hold my hand when we take a walk." Children light up when a parent or other family member pulls them aside and expresses gratitude for the way they're acting. Kind words take only a moment to say, but their echoes last and last.

Today

I'll say kind words to my child.

October 29

"Education is all a matter of building bridges."
Ralph Ellison

Children enjoy learning more when we build bridges to what they learn. Suppose you're teaching your toddler about colors. Take him or her outside and show how the colors can be seen in the everyday world. "See the blue sky? Look at the green leaves! The flowers are red and yellow." If your preschooler is learning to write the alphabet, point out how the letters form words. "M-O-M spells *mom*. D-A-D spells *dad*. Let's sound out the word *cat*." Building bridges is about making connections, and these connections help learning come to life.

Today
I'll help my child make connections.

October 30

"I suppose leadership at one time meant muscles; but today it means getting along with people."
Indira Gandhi

Compassion, empathy, the ability to *listen, communicate,* and *compromise* — these are skills of many of the world's great leaders. They're also the skills that prominent people in your community — religious leaders, business owners, and those in the fields of education and social services — may hold. You can think of young children as "leaders in training." As they grow and learn to get along with others, acknowledge and praise their interpersonal strengths. You might say, "That was really neat how you included Kyra's brother in your game." Assist children with their weaknesses as well. Words like "I understand that you don't want to share your crayons, but think about how that makes your friend feel" can help young children see that their actions have an impact on others.

Today
I'll help children interact positively.

October 31

**"The good news for parents
is that they can take an active role
in keeping their children safe."**
Heather Paul, Ph.D.

Halloween is a fun holiday for young children. Their imaginations soar as they picture themselves wearing a costume and getting treats from the neighbors. Help keep the holiday safe by following these basic tips: (1) trick-or-treat during daylight or dusk hours, (2) examine goodies before you allow children to eat them, and (3) choose costumes without masks (which can impair vision) or long tails (which can cause a child to trip). If you use common sense and accompany young children at all times, you'll provide a safe, memorable, and happy Halloween.

Today
I'll keep Halloween safe.

November 1

"I cannot live without books."
Thomas Jefferson

Today is National Author's Day—a day that honors and celebrates people who write books. If your child is part of a preschool or childcare program, invite a children's author or illustrator to show his or her book and talk about how books are made. (You can often find the names of local children's authors by contacting your library or bookstore.) Another option is to take your child to a local bookstore that's sponsoring an author visit or a read-aloud hour for young children. Check the entertainment section of your newspaper, or contact a library or bookstore for dates.

Today
I'll plan for my children to meet an author.

November 2

"The goal is to teach the child *self*-discipline, *self*-direction, and *self*-responsibility."
Louise Hart, Ph.D.

Young children have to be taught right and wrong, but more importantly, they need to learn how to figure out the difference *themselves*. If your child runs out to the sidewalk the moment you step outside, use this as an opportunity to point out why the behavior is inappropriate. You might say, "It's not safe to run out there by yourself. The bigger kids are riding their bikes, and you could get knocked over." When you explain why the behavior needs to change, young children better understand what is and what isn't appropriate. And gradually, they learn how to think for themselves—an important move toward self-discipline.

Today
When I discipline, I'll explain why.

November 3

**"Nothing is particularly hard
if you divide it into small jobs."**
Henry Ford

Tying shoes is a tough task for young children. (Luckily, Velcro was invented.) If your preschooler wants to learn to tie, you've got a chance to teach him or her about breaking down a task into manageable steps. Begin by simply showing how to tie—and talk about your plan to start small. Next, concentrate on how to cross the shoelaces like the letter X. Later, focus on putting the end of one lace through the X and pulling tight. Once this skill is mastered, help your child make a "bunny ear" (loop) with one lace; when you think he or she is ready, demonstrate wrapping the bunny ear with the other lace. At first, it may seem as if there are too many laces to handle—and then not enough once your child gets to the loop stage. Tying can be trying, but your child will eventually get the hang of it!

Today
I'll practice tying with a preschooler.

SOCIAL COMPETENCIES
ASSET #32: PLANNING AND DECISION MAKING

November 4

**"We tell [parents and children]
that they are part of something great:
the family of all people."**
Sarah Spence

Sarah and Welcome Spence wanted to help build a better community. Their idea was to organize a Dad-Son Day at a local park, giving fathers and sons an opportunity to play games, talk, and have fun. Turns out, the event was a success, and the Spences were inspired to put even more effort into community building. Maybe you have memories of growing up in a close-knit community that felt warm and welcoming—or maybe you've vowed that your children won't grow up in a place like the one you remember as a child. Either way, you've got feelings about the kind of community you want for your children. Like the Spences, you can help people in your community come together—what might you do?

Today
I'll focus on community building.

November 5

**"Have you grown to the point where you can
unflinchingly stand up for the right . . .
whether it makes you popular or unpopular?"**
Booker T. Washington

What do young children in your community need?
Do they have challenging schools? Enough high-
quality childcare centers? Safe playgrounds and
parks? Access to good medical care? Standing up for
young children—and those who care for and teach
them—can mean doing something big or small. You
might write an editorial for your local paper, attend
educational conferences, or coordinate the cleanup
of a playground in your area. You might ask your
employer to cover a portion of childcare expenses
or to donate money to a nonprofit organization that
works on behalf of young children. Take a stand any
way you can.

Today
I'll stand up for young children.

POSITIVE VALUES
ASSET #28: FAMILY VALUES INTEGRITY

November 6

"Children need to hear what they're doing well."
Marianne Daniels Garber, Ph.D.

When you spend a lot of time with young children, you may feel as if every other word out of your mouth is no. Of course, no is unavoidable when a toddler grabs an electrical cord or a preschooler is about to jump off the jungle gym, but children who hear constant nos may begin to tune out the word. Make an effort to save the word no for when you really need it. You might correct a child by saying, "Please put that down," or "I need you to stop doing that." And say *yes* as often as possible by focusing on what children are doing well. "Sure you can help hold the baby," or "I like the way you carry your plate so carefully" can help a young child feel supported and encouraged.

Today

I'll say yes more than no.

November 7

**"Autumn: wheezy, sneezy, freezy.
Winter: slippy, drippy, nippy."**
Anonymous

November, in many parts of the country, can be a "mixed bag" of weather. Some days are crisp and sunny, while others are breezy and wet. Toward the end of the month, you may even see snow. No matter what the weather, get outdoors with your children and enjoy yourselves. Rake up fallen leaves and then invite some children in your neighborhood to jump in the piles of red, orange, and gold. To make sure this activity is safe, remove any large sticks, put the rakes away before the children arrive, and ask everyone to take turns (to avoid collisions). You may even want to have the children's parents join in the fun, and then gather for some warm apple cider afterward.

Today

I'll keep a close eye on children as we play outside.

November 8

**"It does not require many words
to speak the truth."**
Chief Joseph

You want children to tell the truth with a simple yes or no, but what you get may be more complex. Young children may make up stories or excuses to protect themselves, not realizing that adults can see right through these lies. In fact, it's not unusual for a young child to do something right in front of you and deny it. What should you do? Don't ask your child if he or she has told you the truth—this could simply lead to another lie, compounding the problem. Instead, reinforce the idea that honesty is important and mistakes are okay. You might say, "I like hearing the truth, not lies. It's okay to make mistakes, but it's not okay to lie about them."

Today
I'll get to the truth.

November 9

"Having children is the number-one impetus people have for returning or turning to a church or a synagogue."
Dean R. Hoge, Ph.D.

Researchers have found an interesting trend: many people stop attending a congregation when they're older teenagers—and many start going back once they're adults and have children of their own. Why is this? Some people want to pass on their religious upbringing to their children; others want to give their children a spiritual and moral grounding; still others are seeking community. To encourage your children to grow up in a congregation *and* stick with it—even through the teen years—you can create meaningful religious traditions for your family. For example, go out for breakfast after early morning services, light a candle as you say a mealtime prayer, or get to know another family in the congregation and do things together when services are over.

Today
I'll create a religious tradition we'll stick with.

CONSTRUCTIVE USE OF TIME
ASSET #19: RELIGIOUS COMMUNITY

November 10

**"Walk through the crisis together,
recognizing pain as something you go through,
not something you end with."**
Karen Dockrey

Karen Dockrey is a parent of two daughters: one who has leukemia and one who has severe hearing loss. If you have or know a child with a chronic medical condition, a disability, or a learning difficulty, you can help him or her to make the best of the situation—even if it's one of the hardest things you'll ever do in life. While her family spends time in the hospital, Karen Dockrey makes up games for all of them to play. She also encourages her two daughters to express their frustration, anger, and sadness as often as needed. By supporting children as they experience progress and setbacks, you teach them that life is about ups and downs—and that you'll be there for them every step of the way.

Today
**I'll help children handle
any long-term issues they face.**

November 11

"Families that support the emotional well-being and growth of their members combine two almost opposite traits. They combine discipline with spontaneity, rules with freedom, high expectations with unstinting love."

Mihaly Csikszentmihalyi, Ph.D.

Your children need a balance of opposites: dependence and independence; time alone and time with people; stimulating activities and opportunities to simply hang out; high expectations and never-ending support. How do you challenge yet support young children at the same time? You might, for example, encourage your baby to stand up on her own by holding her hand, and then let go for short periods of time. Or you might help your toddler or preschooler learn to kick his legs in the water by providing an inner tube that keeps him afloat as you safely move him around the pool. Parenting, like life itself, is a fine balancing act.

Today
I'll support my children as I challenge them.

November 12

"Hacer bien nunca se pierde."
"Good deeds are never lost."
Southwestern Spanish proverb

Each year, the children at Peachtree United Methodist Church in Atlanta, Georgia, raise money in support of the Heifer Project, an organization that gives families in developing countries a way to feed themselves and become self-reliant. The three- to five-year-olds involved in the Peachtree service project choose an animal to donate to a family who lives far away. So far, they've funded two goats— Velveeta and Feta—who cost a total of $240. The goats can provide nutritious dairy products for the families who raise them. Carolyn Brooks, who directs this program with United Methodist Church, says that the children are "learning an important lesson about life—that sharing is indeed a gift." What might your children do?

Today
I'll think of new ways to help children serve.

November 13

*"Tell me, what is it you plan to do
with your one wild and precious life?"*
Mary Oliver

Why wait for your child to enter elementary or middle school to learn about careers? When your preschooler—or even your toddler—shows interest in a particular game, toy, or type of play, you can show him or her the bigger picture. If your child enjoys playing "store," see if your local grocer will give the two of you a tour. Go watch trainers at a zoo, gardeners at a local nursery, or construction workers around town. You'll not only give your child aspirations but also increase his or her knowledge and experience.

Today
I'll teach a child about a career.

POSITIVE IDENTITY
ASSET #39: SENSE OF PURPOSE

November 14

**"When I've asked my kids about the times
they remember best as a family, they don't talk
about when we were flying around accomplishing
things, but the times we were just hanging out."**
Marilyn Ruman

Need to slow down and spend some leisure time
with your family? How about having a movie night
(or afternoon)? Take your children to the library or
the video store to choose a few family-friendly
videos to bring home. Sit on the couch together and
sip from juice boxes as you watch. You may even
want to prepare a healthy snack ahead of time, such
as cut-up fruit or homemade trail mix that includes
raisins and dry cereal. Most important of all, cuddle
up together and just enjoy being close.

Today
I'll organize movie time at home.

November 15

**"Adults who work
with young children and their families
are key to providing high-quality programs."**
*National Assocation for the Education
of Young Children (NAEYC)*

A supportive program is a caring place for children
and adults. Yet, many early-childhood programs
suffer from high staff turnover. When teachers and
caregivers aren't happy, they leave, and when
parents aren't happy, they pull their children out of
a program. Your childcare center can buck the
trend by being a place that is creative, caring, and
welcoming—all things that money can't buy. Invite
caregivers, teachers, and parents to form commit-
tees to address issues and support each other.
Become NAEYC accredited, which attracts families
and instills a sense of pride in staff members. When
caregivers and teachers feel that they belong, they
want to stay. When children feel cared for, they
want to keep coming back.

Today
I'll help create a more caring program.

SUPPORT
ASSET #5: CARING OUT-OF-HOME CLIMATE

November 16

**"King Bidgood's in the bathtub,
and he won't get out!
Oh, who knows what to do?"**
Audrey Wood

In the picture book *King Bidgood's in the Bathtub,* the king refuses to get out of the tub, so the duke joins him and the two go fishing. Soon the queen hops in for a bit of lunch. This parody has a ring of familiarity because, like the king, many young children resist getting out of the water—just as they resist getting in! How do you keep your cool when children refuse to cooperate? The trick is to make the next activity seem just as fun as the current one. Your child doesn't want to get in the tub? Tempt him or her with a "spooky bath" taken by candlelight. Now your child doesn't want to get out? Encourage him or her with a promise of a favorite bedtime story and plenty of snuggling.

Today
I'll be creative about transitions.

November 17

**"Don't fight in front of your children,
because it changes who they are."**
Dr. Phil McGraw

When parents model peaceful behaviors, young
children feel calmer and more secure. The opposite
is true as well. If you argue or yell in front of your
children, they feel frightened. They sense that their
world isn't a safe place after all. To keep this from
happening, make a pact with your spouse or partner not to fight in front of the children. Agree
on a plan that you can put into effect when an
argument begins to brew. You might signal each
other by saying, "Let's take a break and think about
this. Can we talk after putting the kids to bed?"
Keep in mind that young children learn about emotions—and how to handle them—by watching what
you do.

Today
I won't fight in front of my children.

SOCIAL COMPETENCIES
ASSET #33: INTERPERSONAL SKILLS

November 18

"Learning about a variety of roles and finding role models for a girl or a boy means knowing a lot of different kinds of people—men and women— at home, in school, and in the community."

Margaret Mead

Eileen Kreek was a single parent when she adopted Carlos. Concerned that she couldn't provide male role models for him, she was thrilled when a man in her congregation, Mr. Turner, said that he'd like to get to know her son better. Mr. Turner and his wife now had an empty nest, and they missed spending time with children. Soon he and Carlos were going swimming and to the circus, or simply playing. When the boy started kindergarten, Mr. Turner cheered him on and continues to be a major source of support. Eileen Kreek was lucky: when she needed a role model for her son, one appeared. If you'd like to find a role model, your congregation or community center can be a great place to start looking.

Today
I'll continue seeking role models for my child.

November 19

"Creativity is seeing something that doesn't exist already."
Michele Shea

The weather isn't cooperating, and you're stuck inside with a young child who's bored with all of his or her toys. Now what? Get creative. Pull a small step ladder up to the sink, fill it with bubbly water and plastic plates and cups, and have your child do the dishes for a while. Find empty cardboard tubes (from wrapping paper or paper towels, for example) and let your child use them as tunnels for small cars. Paint a large cardboard box and make it into a new home for a doll or stuffed animal. Or use this time together to put photos in albums and frames. Let an indoor day be a creative day.

Today
I'll make inside time fun.

CONSTRUCTIVE USE OF TIME
ASSET #17: CREATIVE ACTIVITIES

November 20

**"I may not be totally perfect,
but parts of me are excellent."**
Ashleigh Brilliant

When an infant or adoptive child first arrives, it's not unusual to feel that he or she is pure perfection. You can't imagine any child more beautiful or wonderful. By toddlerhood, you're wondering what happened to your "perfect" child, and by the time he or she is a preschooler, you've long given up hope. This is a *good* thing. Having expectations of perfection in children lowers their self-esteem by providing expectations they can never live up to—perfection simply doesn't exist. Instead, show children the beauty of their flaws—and don't be shy about showing yours.

Today
I'll celebrate our imperfections.

November 21

"One thing everybody in the world wants and needs is friendliness."
William E. Holler

Today is World Hello Day. The sponsors suggest that every person should greet ten other people to help make the world a friendlier place. Why stop at ten, though? Go out of your way to greet every person you see as you walk through your neighborhood, local park, or community. Encourage your child to wave and say hi, too. When you say hello to others and reach out in this way, your world becomes bigger and your community feels smaller.

Today
I'll greet the people I meet.

November 22

"Many people don't know how to get a hold
of their sense of self, that sense that says, 'I *am*—
and I need to strengthen this me.'"
Sidney Poitier

When he was young, Sidney Poitier dreamed of becoming an actor. When he flubbed his lines while trying out for his first acting job, the director told him to stop wasting his time and get a job as a dishwasher. But Poitier was raised to believe in himself, so he continued to work on his dream. Not only did Poitier become an actor, he became the first (and, for now, the only) black person to receive an Oscar for Best Actor. When you show your children that you believe in them, they begin to believe in themselves. They learn to have faith in their future and their power to be whatever they want to be in life. What a wonderful legacy.

Today
I'll help children believe in themselves.

November 23

"Young children learn about the world,
including what is safe and what is not,
through firsthand experience."
Charles Flatter, Ed.D.

November is Child Safety and Protection Month.
Although children of preschool age are more independent, they still don't fully grasp the dangers
around them. Preschoolers may get into matches or
cigarette lighters, or try to open cleaning products
or paint cans. They may climb on a bookshelf to
reach a book, or they may even attempt sliding
down a banister. Continue to be vigilant by closely
supervising preschool-age children and keeping
unsafe items out of their reach.

Today
I'll look for safety risks at home.

EMPOWERMENT
ASSET #10: SAFETY

November 24

"Gratitude helps you to grow and expand."
Eileen Caddy

Thanksgiving is a time to count our blessings. Whether you celebrate this U.S. holiday or not, help young children think about the many good things in their lives. In your classroom or childcare center, talk about what being thankful means. You can help the children make a horn of plenty out of construction paper and fill it with paper fruits and vegetables; on each item write one thing that each child in the group is grateful for (for example, "my family," "my home," or "good friends"). By counting what they're thankful for, children learn to appreciate the meaning of this holiday—and the importance of giving thanks.

Today
I'll help children give thanks.

November 25

**"Community can arise naturally
when people come together
for the purpose of helping others."**
Portuguese proverb

Maybe you've heard or read stories of families who spend Thanksgiving or some other day serving a meal at a shelter—and maybe you've thought about doing this yourself. You might also consider going to a home for senior citizens to spend time with people whose families can't be there. While many of us are inspired to help around the holidays, we can be of service at *any* time of the year. Consider what the Cohn family of Massachusetts decided to do: even though they have four children under the age of five, they open their busy home to families of patients traveling to Boston for medical care. The Cohns, and others like them, show us that helping people brings families and communities together.

Today
I'll care for others with my child by my side.

November 26

"Sisters and brothers share a special lifelong bond."
Diane Crispell

Siblings share a special bond—one that may often seem on the verge of breaking! Brothers and sisters tend to argue *a lot* over little things—even when the relationship is close. What's at the root of these squabbles? Often, it's jealousy. Children feel that their position in the family is threatened if a sibling seems to get more attention. This is especially true when a new baby arrives: the older child may suddenly act younger by crying frequently, sucking a thumb, or wetting the bed more often. You can help by recognizing these jealous feelings and showing children how to handle them. You might say, "I see that you feel sad. Is it because Daddy's feeding the baby? What can I do to help?" Give your child a hug and reassurance that you don't love him or her any less.

Today
I'll help siblings get along.

November 27

**"Be careful going in search of adventure—
it's ridiculously easy to find."**
William Least Heat Moon

Places that we, as adults, consider almost run-of-the-mill, can be very exciting for toddlers or preschoolers. Take the car wash, for example. Young children are often fascinated by the water, suds, and giant brushes. How about the grocery store? Young children may enjoy looking at all of the different foods and people; enhance the excitement by letting children touch the fruits and vegetables that you put in your cart. A bowling alley can be a source of adventure for a child—there's so much to do, see, and hear. Consider other places that might prove interesting: the airport, the bakery, an elevator or escalator, your workplace, a barn, or a hardware store.

Today

I'll seek a simple adventure.

CONSTRUCTIVE USE OF TIME
ASSET #18: OUT-OF-HOME ACTIVITIES

November 28

**"Remember that your parents did
the best they could
and that you are doing the best you can."**
Jean Illsley Clarke

What happens if you and your child are visiting your mom and dad, and they give you unasked-for parenting advice? "You should put him in the playpen more often." "Why are you feeding her food from a jar—I made all your baby food from scratch!" *"You* were toilet-trained at fifteen months." Although well intentioned, such comments can feel a lot like interference. Gently tell Grandma or Grandpa that you're not only an adult now but also a *parent.* You might say, "Mom, we don't agree on this issue. Let's change the subject," or "Dad, I feel I know best when it comes to raising my child." Remember—and remind others—that you're in charge and you're doing the best you can.

Today
I'll remember that I'm the parent.

November 29

"Child-restraint systems . . .
protect the nation's most precious resource—
the children who represent our future."
National Highway
Traffic Safety Administration (NHTSA)

A large part of our responsibility as adults is keeping children safe. From day one, young children need to be buckled into approved, properly installed car seats. These child-restraint systems are the best and only way to protect children during a fender-bender or a more severe accident, yet many adults fail to use them properly. In fact, a 1996 study by the NHTSA found that 79 percent of adults use child seats incorrectly. Be sure that you've followed the instructions for safe installation of a child-restraint system, including putting it in the *back* seat of the vehicle, facing it in the correct direction, and buckling the safety harness.

Today
I'll double check my child's car seat.

November 30

"Motivation is everything."
Lee Iacocca

Have you ever watched what happens when toddlers lose their interest in an activity? They may express boredom by crying, whining, or throwing something in frustration. When young children no longer feel motivated, they're like a flat tire—stalled and stuck. As their caregivers, we need to stay one step ahead of them by noticing what keeps them interested and what makes them go flat. Be sure to offer a variety of indoor and outdoor activities, and switch gears as often as needed. You may even want to "rotate" toys and games: put certain ones away for a week or so, and then bring them out again to maintain their appeal.

Today
I'll find creative ways to keep children interested.

December 1

"The only tired I was, was tired of giving in."
Rosa Parks

December 1 in the U.S. is Rosa Parks Day, the anniversary of the day in 1955 when Rosa, a black woman, refused to move to the back of the bus when a white man asked for her seat. Many people think she protested because she was weary after a long day's work—but Rosa Parks had decided to take a stand against mistreatment. Taking a stand is never easy, but it's how you make a difference. What might you stand up for on behalf of young children, who don't have the power or ability to stand up for themselves? More affordable childcare? Safer neighborhoods? Stronger communities?

Today
I'll be a voice for children.

EMPOWERMENT
ASSET #7: COMMUNITY VALUES CHILDREN

December 2

"We need a great many people who are willing to devote themselves to the care of children who are not their own."
Margaret Mead

Want to make a difference in the lives of young children you don't know? There are lots of ways to connect with children. You might serve at your local community center, YMCA/YWCA, or library. You might do a craft project with a group of toddlers or arrange for a class of preschoolers to tour your place of employment. You might spend time holding and singing to premature babies at a local hospital. There are so many ways to reach out to children. Get started by making a list of ways you'd like to help.

Today
I'll become involved in another child's life.

December 3

*"A good head and a good heart are always
a formidable combination."*
Nelson Mandela

How do you build integrity in young children?
One way is to help them notice how others are feeling. For example, if your preschooler points to a
crying child, ask, "What do you think he's feeling?"
After your child has said "Sad," follow up by asking, "What can we do to help him?" Encourage
your child to give the other child a hug or a toy. If
your toddler colors a picture and wants to send it
to someone, help him or her act on that impulse.
You might say, "Great! Who should we mail it to?"
Guiding young children in these ways encourages
them to use their head and their heart—both of
which help children to do the right thing and act on
their beliefs.

Today
I'll help my young child build integrity.

December 4

**"Shoot for the moon. Even if you miss it,
you will land among the stars."**
Les Brown

Young children have lots of ambition. They want to
dress up like a grown-up they admire or build the
world's most amazing secret hideaway. What kind
of help might you give? Perhaps you could find
large boxes and help your child paint them to look
like tunnels and caves. Perhaps you might go
through your closets for old clothes, shoes, acces-
sories, or jewelry, so your child can dress up as your
twin. When you help young children reach — or
exceed — their expectations, they feel not only
satisfied but also proud.

Today
I'll help a child reach a goal.

December 5

"This is one of the glories of man, the inventiveness of the human mind and the human spirit: whenever life doesn't seem to give an answer, we create one."
Lorraine Hansberry

When Amy Jaffee Barzach took her children to the playground near her home in West Hartford, Connecticut, she noticed a child in a wheelchair, sitting and watching, unable to play on the equipment. This bothered Amy, but when she learned that federal standards for new playgrounds required only a ramp for accessibility, she wondered how children with disabilities could play on the equipment once they reached it. Determined to help, she raised money and recruited volunteers to create a playground with waist-high sandboxes, a ramp-accessible tree house, and more, so children of *all* abilities could play side by side. How might you make your playground, school, classroom, or childcare center even more accessible and child-friendly?

Today
I'll create a solution that benefits all children.

December 6

**"A child's conduct will reflect the ways
of his parents."**
Arnold Lobel

You've heard the old sayings "Like father, like son,"
"Like mother, like daughter." Young children often
act in ways that mimic the adults around them.
Everyday actions that you may hardly be aware of
can have an impact on your child. For example, if
you yell or slam doors when you're angry, your
child may do the same. On the other hand, if you
take a deep breath and count to ten when you're
mad, your child will learn a more positive way of
coping with strong feelings. It helps to notice what
you do and how you act. If necessary, make some
changes—for your child's benefit and your own.

Today
I'll consider how I act.

December 7

"Preguntando se llega a Roma."
"Questions will get us to what we want to learn."
Southwestern Spanish proverb

We learn about others by asking questions. In this way, we get a sense of people's personalities and tastes. Asking questions is a good way to get to know young children better. Ask them about their likes and dislikes: favorite color, best-loved toy, best friend, best food, worst food, and favorite place to go. By getting personal with young children, you show them that you take an interest in who they are. They'll see the value of being curious about other people and asking questions to find out what they want to know.

Today
I'll ask children about themselves.

December 8

**"It's easy to fear your child is going
to hate you forever. Just acknowledge
her feelings for what they are—and move on."**
Fran Litman

Sometimes your child may not want to spend time
with you. Your child may only want to be with
Mom and not Dad (or the other way around).
Experts say that children between the ages of one
and three often favor one parent over the other. At
preschool age, children may even say, "I don't like
you!" and point out that they prefer another adult
instead. While it hurts to be rejected, know that
your child's resistance actually is healthy—it means
that your child is forming a primary attachment to
another person. If your child resists you, honor his
or her feelings but don't back off completely. Find
an activity that your child will enjoy doing with you
and slowly reconnect.

Today
I'll be patient if my child resists being with me.

December 9

**"We, as human beings, must be willing
to accept people who are different from ourselves."**
Barbara Jordan

Everybody is different, and young children often notice (and loudly comment on) these differences while in public. They may ask frank questions, such as, "Why is that man in a wheelchair?" Or "Why are the people in that family all different colors?" Your first impulse may be to shush a child or say, "Don't be rude," but this doesn't lead to understanding. Instead, calmly point out that people have different bodies and faces. Let the child know that these differences are what make each person special or unique. If you want, talk about the questions again when you have a private moment with the child.

Today
I'll teach acceptance.

SOCIAL COMPETENCIES
ASSET #34: CULTURAL COMPETENCE

December 10

"If you take time to talk together each day, you'll never become strangers."
Leo Buscaglia

As parents, you may devote so much time to taking care of your children that you don't have much time left over for each other. Your conversations may often consist of: "Aimee needs a bath tonight," or "Can you feed the baby?" Although you have children, you're still two people who need each other and enjoy spending time together. Your relationship as a couple doesn't have to be put on the back burner. Make time to be alone together and talk—even about little things like how your day went. Talk about the big things, too: your dreams, your aims, your values. Conversations can keep you in touch with each other, no matter how busy or hectic life gets.

Today
I'll remember I'm a partner, too.

December 11

"The world is a wonderful place when you're young."

E. B. White

Some young children embrace their world. Before you know it, your baby might be crawling up and down the stairs alone, or your toddler may start jumping off the furniture. The goal is to keep a close eye on children to make sure these explorations don't pose too much of a risk. On the other hand, some children are naturally more hesitant or cautious. If your child resists trying new things, you might encourage small challenges, such as turning somersaults or tasting new foods. Gradually, your child will feel more comfortable with trying something new — and will learn to embrace the wonderful sense of accomplishment this can lead to.

Today

I'll encourage risks that help children learn and grow.

Commitment to Learning
Asset #22: Children Are Engaged in Learning

December 12

> **"Religious rituals and teachings are only meaningful when they point us toward the connections with all life, human and divine."**
> *Jean Grasso Fitzpatrick*

Which religious rituals are important to pass on to children? Which religious teachings are essential? These are highly personal questions, and each person will answer them differently. Some families keep sacred objects in view to remind them of their spiritual beliefs. Other families light candles on certain religious holidays. And still others pray each night before bed. You may want to talk to your young child about the meaning of rituals and teachings, such as songs, special foods, holiday celebrations, and religious clothing or objects. If you don't already have such traditions, your family may want to discuss some to try.

Today
**I'll think about rituals
I may want to teach my children.**

December 13

"A good start marks the beginning of hope."
David Hamburg, Ph.D.

When a baby is born, doctors and nurses work to make sure he or she is breathing, eating, and digesting well. In the next six months, frequent medical check-ups help ensure that the baby is developing on schedule. These measures are designed to give children a healthy start in life. Young children also need a good *emotional* start. You can help by responding to babies in caring ways; if they fuss, pick them up, rub them gently, or speak in soothing tones. When you hold, rock, cuddle, nurture, and play with babies, you teach them that they'll be cared for now and in the future.

Today
I'll give a baby what he or she needs.

POSITIVE IDENTITY
ASSET #40: POSITIVE VIEW OF PERSONAL FUTURE

December 14

**"Children need your presence
more than your presents."**
Jesse Jackson

Young children feel immensely proud when their
preschool or childcare center holds an event that
parents can attend. Holiday programs, for example,
provide a wonderful opportunity for parents to
observe their children singing or playing simple
instruments. The children may wear ear-to-ear
grins as they perform the songs they've rehearsed
for so long. Make a point of attending these important events—bring a camera or video camera, if you
can. At these gatherings, you can meet your child's
closest friends, get to know other parents, and show
your support for teachers and caregivers.

Today
I'll show up for my child.

December 15

**"Neighbors can and should
work together to create an environment
that does not tolerate family violence."**
Stephanie Mann

We may think of neighborhood crime as burglary or vandalism. But what about family violence? We may want to close our eyes and ears and pretend it doesn't exist—but it does. The U.S. Advisory Board on Child Abuse and Neglect says, "Child maltreatment is most likely to occur in families under stress who lack support from their neighbors." Is your neighborhood keeping an eye out for this problem? As neighbors and community members, what might you do to support each other in times of need?

Today
I'll learn more about signs of abuse or neglect.

BOUNDARIES AND EXPECTATIONS
ASSET #13: NEIGHBORHOOD BOUNDARIES

December 16

"Just the knowledge that a good book is awaiting one at the end of the day makes the day happier."
Kathleen Norris

There's nothing like a good book to create a sense of anticipation and adventure. Actress Gwyneth Paltrow knows this, so for her birthday, she asked her friends not to bring fancy presents—just a copy of their favorite book. At one point in her life when she felt uncertain, a friend gave her a big cardboard box full of his favorite books for her to read, and she remembers this as one of her favorite presents of all. Help your child see that books truly *are* wonderful gifts. Encourage a love of books by creating a private reading nook with a soft beanbag chair, a light, a stuffed animal to hold close, and of course, lots and lots of books.

Today
I'll help a child treasure a book.

December 17

**"There is so much to be done,
and we are the ones to get it done.
You can play a role in your community. . . .
We have to help our kids one at a time."**

Colin Powell

The Owens Corning Newark plant is one of the larger employers in Newark, Ohio, with 2,000 workers. To promote service to others, the company allows hourly employees to take off one paid hour each week to mentor children at a nearby elementary school. According to department manager Al Ernest, "A lot of the hourly factory workers have such low self-esteem. They don't think they can mentor kids. They think, 'I'm just a factory worker.' But . . . they [soon] see they have a lot to give." Children respond when grown-ups give them their time and attention. Any caring person can become a mentor, tutor, volunteer, or role model—how about you?

Today
I'll think about how I can serve children.

EMPOWERMENT
ASSET #9: SERVICE TO OTHERS

December 18

"Repetition does not transform a lie into a truth."
Franklin D. Roosevelt

When young children get caught in a lie, they may hold fast to their fib, repeating that they didn't play with your watch, leave the refrigerator door open, or spill water all over the floor. It doesn't seem to matter if the lie is big or small—some children will maintain their innocence as if somehow repeating it makes it true. You may become frustrated with this continued battle. The solution? Don't let it *become* a battle. Remain calm and let your child know that he or she isn't trapped by a lie. Explain and model that it's never too late to tell the truth.

Today
I'll stay calm if my child lies.

December 19

**"Television can give us so much,
except the time to think."**

Bernice Buresh

Young children not only observe the adults in their
lives to see how conflicts are resolved but also the
characters on television and in movies. Do you keep
tabs on what your children are watching? Sit down
with them and make sure that what's on TV or the
VCR is appropriate for young children. Are the conflicts realistic? Is there more violence than you realized? Are the characters solving problems in ways
that young children can model—or not? Pay special
attention to slapstick humor in cartoons and other
shows—you may want to limit children's exposure
to this. Take a moment to talk to your children
about what they're seeing and suggest more peaceful ways for the characters to work things out.

Today
**I'll watch and discuss a show
or a movie with a child.**

December 20

> "In every community, there is work to be done.
> In every nation, there are wounds to heal.
> In every heart, there is the power to do it."
> *Marianne Williamson*

December is Human Rights Month, an excellent time to talk with young children about issues of equality and justice. During this holiday month, you may also be discussing the importance of giving. If you'd like to bring these lessons together, consider having your family sponsor a child through Pearl S. Buck International, a nonsectarian, humanitarian assistance organization dedicated to improving the quality of life for children *(www.pearl-s-buck.org/psbi/)*. Your contribution will assist a child and his or her family with healthcare, education, and more. In return, your family will receive not only a photo and information about the child you sponsor—but also the satisfaction that you're doing something concrete to help.

Today
I'll consider sponsoring a child.

December 21

**"Teaching kids to count is fine,
but teaching them what counts is best."**
Bob Talbert

When searching for childcare or a preschool for your young child, you may look carefully at the program's "academics." How will the teachers help prepare your child for kindergarten? Will your child learn letters, numbers, colors, and shapes? But perhaps even more important is finding out what else is taught. How do the teachers help children learn to resolve conflicts? Get along? Use their words? Share? Be kind to each other? Help and serve others? It's the answers to these types of questions that show how well a center or school prepares children for kindergarten and beyond.

Today
**I'll notice what counts
at a preschool or childcare center.**

December 22

**"We all have ability.
The difference is how we use it."**
Stevie Wonder

Some young children master language quickly, while others are more physically coordinated. Some young children draw well, while others have a way of making friends easily. Each child has different strengths and abilities. Have you noticed a skill your child has? If so, challenge him or her to develop this ability. If your preschooler is a budding artist, let him experiment with new supplies, such as chalk or colored pencils. If your toddler loves creative movement, encourage her to walk on her tiptoes or spin around. Challenging young children to discover and improve on their skills helps them to grow and succeed.

Today
I'll give a child an extra challenge.

December 23

**"I not only use all the brains I have,
but all I can borrow."**
Woodrow Wilson

Have you ever seen a toddler cleverly move a chair
or a footstool to grasp something out of reach? Have
you ever heard a preschooler describe an unexpected
way to make medicine taste better? Young children
often have creative minds that aren't limited by an
adult's perception of what's "sensible" or "realistic."
Your inclination may be to say, "That won't work
because . . . " Instead, let children imagine possibilities; show them how valuable this kind of creative
thinking is. You may even want to ask a child for
help the next time you've got a problem. He or she
may be able to tell you how to help the baby quiet
down, for example, or how to fix the broken plate.
(But if not, the child's idea may put a smile on your
face and give you a good story to share later on.)

Today
I'll be open to a young child's solutions.

Empowerment
Asset #8: Children Are Given Useful Roles

December 24

"There is no place like home."
L. Frank Baum

Some people speak longingly of their childhood home, a place filled with warm memories, the smells of their favorite foods, and laughter. Often, these strong attachments to a home are more about connections to a caring family. Whether you live in a house or an apartment, whether you rent or own, your home can be a place that's warm and inviting for children. But you don't have to fill your home with *things*, such as expensive toys or games. Instead, create a place of love, laughter, and warm conversation. Help young children feel at home by holding them close, playing with them, and talking to them often. These caring actions make the best memories of all.

Today
I'll get close to my children.

December 25

**"Peace is
Everyone trusting
And
Caring for
Each other."**

Rachel Minshall (eighth grader)

Children who grow up in a caring home know they can count on their family. They feel more valued and appreciated, more secure and at peace. Young children watch and learn from the example you set. Be sure to treat other people in loving, caring ways, especially when you're around young children —and not just during the holiday season, but all through the year.

Today
I'll be peaceful and caring.

December 26

"Imagination is more important than knowledge."
Albert Einstein

Albert Einstein is remembered for his achievements in the world of knowledge, but it was the world of the imagination that gave him his start. His uncles, Jacob Einstein and Caesar Koch, encouraged an interest in science and math by giving young Albert creative activities, including teaching him to play the violin. You too can encourage creativity and imagination by exposing young children to music, to art, and to stories and poetry. Show them library books that contain the work of famous artists and writers; read them poems that rhyme or don't rhyme; take them to a concert featuring holiday music. Creative activities like these help children's imaginations to grow.

Today
I'll stir a child's imagination.

December 27

"Routines involving wake-up times, mealtimes, nap times, and bedtimes are soothing and help children learn to make transitions."
Nancy Leffert, Ph.D.

You take care of your children by helping them to eat healthy foods, get exercise, take naps, and learn to sleep through the night. Daily routines show your children how much you care—and how important it is to take care of themselves. Routines also let children know what comes next and help make transitions easier. You can help make these daily habits special and fun by talking about them. You might say, "When you eat healthy foods, your body gets stronger," or "Taking a nap gives your body a chance to rest." During bathtime, you might say, "This shampoo will make your hair clean and help it smell good," or "Let's use lots of soap to get all of this dirt off!" Smile and laugh together as you teach your children to stay healthy.

Today
I'll explain the importance of daily routines.

December 28

"We superheroes bruise easily, you know."
***Supergrover, from* Sesame Street**

When Grover (also known as "Supergrover") puts on his cape and heads for the skies, he shows young children the funny side of being a superhero. He bumps into buildings, overestimates what he can do, and falls down—proving that blunders happen to anyone, and even heroes have bad days. As an adult, you're a role model for the children in your life, but this doesn't mean you have to be "super" or "perfect." You can be who you are: someone who has faults like everyone else. Show children that you're okay with goofing up. You might say, "Oops, I blew it. We all make mistakes sometimes." And laugh it off.

Today
I'll remember that I'm only human.

December 29

**"Your well-being is essential
to the well-being of your child."**
Mary Sheedy Kurcinka

Your well-being depends on you. What makes you feel alert and active? Is it going for a run? Reading? Doing a craft? Playing music? Writing in a journal? Cooking? Talking to a good friend? As a parent or caregiver, you often do for others. But what about *you*? Do you ever make time for yourself? Young children notice when you're energized, excited, and content—they also notice when you seem drained. To give them your best each day, spend a little time on yourself. What's one thing you could do today to help yourself feel more alive? Once you decide, go out and do it. You're worth it—and so are your children.

Today
I'll focus on my well-being.

POSITIVE IDENTITY
ASSET #38: SELF-ESTEEM

December 30

> **"The one thing children need most
> in order to grow up happy and secure
> is a close-knit, loving family."**
> *T. Berry Brazelton, M.D.*

Life's pressures and stresses can take a toll on families—especially those with two parents who work outside the home. In response to the stresses and hectic schedules of today's families, a group of parents and child advocates created the organization Family Life 1st, which recommends that families make time together a priority and set limits on their outside activities. (Learn more about these ideas at *www.familylife1st.org*.) By taking time to eat dinner together, hang out at home, and go on outings, families can become closer and more loving—and children grow up feeling more secure. Can your family set aside at least one night a week to be with each other? Unplug the phone, turn off the TV, avoid checking email—and enjoy this uninterrupted time together.

Today
I'll focus on family time.

December 31

"Every intersection in the road of life is an opportunity to make a decision."
Duke Ellington

December 31 is Make Up Your Mind Day—it's also the last day of the year. You may already be reflecting on the past and thinking about your resolutions for the coming year. What hopes do you have for the future? What changes would you like to make or see? What will you make up your mind to do? Consider ways to continue guiding and serving the children in your life. Can you make time with your family even more special and meaningful? Can you resolve to build a stronger community for the children you care for and teach? Today is the day to begin again.

Today
I'll make up my mind about the future.

40 Assets INFANTS Need to Succeed
(Birth to 12 Months)

1. FAMILY SUPPORT. Family life provides high levels of love and support.

2. POSITIVE FAMILY COMMUNICATION. Parents communicate with infants in positive ways. Parents respond immediately to infants and respect their needs.

3. OTHER ADULT RELATIONSHIPS. Parents have support from three or more adults and ask for help when needed. Children receive additional love and comfort from at least one adult other than their parents.

4. CARING NEIGHBORHOOD. Children experience caring neighbors.

5. CARING OUT-OF-HOME CLIMATE. Children are in caring, encouraging environments outside the home.

6. PARENT INVOLVEMENT IN OUT-OF-HOME SITUATIONS. Parents are actively involved in communicating infants' needs to caretakers and others in situations outside the home.

7. COMMUNITY VALUES CHILDREN. The family places infants at the center of family life. Other adults in the community value and appreciate infants.

8. Children Are Given Useful Roles. The family involves infants in family life.

9. Service to Others. Parents serve others in the community.

10. Safety. Children have safe environments at home, in out-of-home settings, and in the neighborhood. This includes childproofing these environments.

11. Family Boundaries. Parents are aware of infants' preferences and adapt the environment and schedule to suit infants' needs. Parents begin setting limits as infants become mobile.

12. Out-of-Home Boundaries. Childcare settings and other out-of-home environments have clear rules and consequences for older infants and consistently provide all infants with appropriate stimulation and enough rest.

13. Neighborhood Boundaries. Neighbors take responsibility for monitoring and supervising children's behavior as they begin to play and interact outside the home.

14. Adult Role Models. Parents and other adults model positive, responsible behavior.

15. Positive Peer Interaction and Influence. Infants observe siblings and other children interacting

in positive ways. They have opportunities to interact with children of various ages.

16. APPROPRIATE EXPECTATIONS FOR GROWTH. Parents have realistic expectations for children's development at this age. Parents encourage development without pushing children beyond their own pace.

17. CREATIVE ACTIVITIES. Parents expose infants to music, art, or other creative aspects of the environment each day.

18. OUT-OF-HOME ACTIVITIES. Parents expose children to limited but stimulating situations outside the home. The family keeps children's needs in mind when attending events.

19. RELIGIOUS COMMUNITY. The family regularly attends religious programs or services while keeping children's needs in mind.

20. POSITIVE, SUPERVISED TIME AT HOME. Parents supervise children at all times and provide predictable, enjoyable routines at home.

21. ACHIEVEMENT EXPECTATION AND MOTIVATION. Family members are motivated to do well at work, at school, and in the community, and model their motivation for children.

22. CHILDREN ARE ENGAGED IN LEARNING. Parents and family members model responsive and attentive attitudes at work, at school, in the community, and at home.

23. STIMULATING ACTIVITY AND HOMEWORK. Parents encourage children to explore and provide stimulating toys that match children's emerging skills. Parents are sensitive to children's dispositions, preferences, and level of development.

24. ENJOYMENT OF LEARNING AND BONDING TO SCHOOL. Parents enjoy learning and model this through their own learning activities.

25. READING FOR PLEASURE. Parents read to infants in enjoyable ways every day.

26. FAMILY VALUES CARING. Parents convey their beliefs about helping others by modeling their helping behaviors.

27. FAMILY VALUES EQUALITY AND SOCIAL JUSTICE. Parents place a high value on promoting social equality, religious tolerance, and reducing hunger and poverty while modeling these beliefs for children.

28. FAMILY VALUES INTEGRITY. Parents act on their convictions, stand up for their beliefs, and communicate and model this in the family.

29. FAMILY VALUES HONESTY. Parents tell the truth and convey their belief in honesty through their actions.

30. FAMILY VALUES RESPONSIBILITY. Parents accept and take personal responsibility.

31. FAMILY VALUES HEALTHY LIFESTYLE. Parents love children, setting the foundation for infants to develop healthy attitudes and beliefs about relationships. Parents model, monitor, and teach the importance of good health habits, and provide good nutritional choices and adequate rest and playtime.

32. PLANNING AND DECISION MAKING. Parents make all safety and care decisions for children and model safe behavior. As children become more independently mobile, parents allow them to make simple choices.

33. INTERPERSONAL SKILLS. Parents model positive, constructive interactions with other people. Parents accept and are responsive to how infants express their feelings, seeing those expressions as cues to infants' needs.

34. CULTURAL COMPETENCE. Parents know and are comfortable with people of different cultural,

racial, and/or ethnic backgrounds, and model this to children.

35. RESISTANCE SKILLS. Parents model resistance skills through their own behavior.

36. PEACEFUL CONFLICT RESOLUTION. Parents behave in acceptable, r   t ways and assist children in developing   s by helping them solve problems wh   ced with challenging or frustrating circu

37. PERSONAL POWER   eel they have control over things that happe   r own lives and model coping skills, demonsu.   .g healthy ways to deal with frustrations and challenges. Parents respond to children so children begin to learn that they have influence ov-   mediate surroundings.

38. SELF-E   its create an environment where chilc   levelop positive self-esteem, giving childrei.   opriate, positive feedback and reinforcement about their skills and competencies.

39. SENSE OF PURPOSE. Parents report that their lives have purpose and demonstrate these beliefs through their behaviors. Infants are curious about the world around them.

40. Positive View of Personal Future. Parents are hopeful and positive about their personal future and work to provide a positive future for children.

40 Assets TODDLERS Need to Succeed (Ages 13 to 35 Months)

1. Family Support. Family life provides high levels of love and support.

2. Positive Family Communication. Parents communicate with toddlers in positive ways. Parents respond to toddlers in a reasonable amount of time and respect their needs.

3. Other Adult Relationships. Parents have support from three or more adults and ask for help when needed. Children receive additional love and comfort from at least one adult other than their parents.

4. Caring Neighborhood. Children experience caring neighbors.

5. Caring Out-of-Home Climate. Children are in caring, encouraging environments outside the home.

6. Parent Involvement in Out-of-Home Situations. Parents are actively involved in helping toddlers succeed in situations outside the home. Parents

communicate toddlers' needs to caretakers outside the home.

7. COMMUNITY VALUES CHILDREN. The family places toddlers at the center of family life and recognizes the need to set limits for toddlers. Other adults in the community value and appreciate toddlers.

8. CHILDREN ARE GIVEN USEFUL ROLES. The family involves toddlers in family life.

9. SERVICE TO OTHERS. Parents serve others in the community.

10. SAFETY. Children have safe environments at home, in out-of-home settings, and in the neighborhood. This includes childproofing these environments.

11. FAMILY BOUNDARIES. Parents are aware of toddlers' preferences and adapt the environment to suit toddlers' needs. Parents set age-appropriate limits for toddlers.

12. OUT-OF-HOME BOUNDARIES. Childcare settings and other out-of-home environments have clear rules and consequences to protect toddlers while consistently providing appropriate stimulation and enough rest.

13. NEIGHBORHOOD BOUNDARIES. Neighbors take responsibility for monitoring and supervising

children's behavior as they begin to play and interact outside the home.

14. ADULT ROLE MODELS. Parents and other adults model positive, responsible behavior.

15. POSITIVE PEER INTERACTION AND INFLUENCE. Toddlers observe siblings and other children interacting in positive ways. They have opportunities to interact with children of various ages.

16. APPROPRIATE EXPECTATIONS FOR GROWTH. Parents have realistic expectations for children's development at this age. Parents encourage development without pushing children beyond their own pace.

17. CREATIVE ACTIVITIES. Parents expose toddlers to music, art, or other creative age-appropriate activities each day.

18. OUT-OF-HOME ACTIVITIES. Parents expose children to limited but stimulating situations outside the home. The family keeps children's needs in mind when attending events.

19. RELIGIOUS COMMUNITY. The family regularly attends religious programs or services while keeping children's needs in mind.

20. Positive, Supervised Time at Home. Parents supervise children at all times and provide predictable, enjoyable routines at home.

21. Achievement Expectation and Motivation. Family members are motivated to do well at work, at school, and in the community, and model their motivation for children.

22. Children Are Engaged in Learning. Parents and family members model responsive and attentive attitudes at work, at school, in the community, and at home.

23. Stimulating Activity and Homework. Parents encourage children to explore and provide stimulating toys that match children's emerging skills. Parents are sensitive to children's dispositions, preferences, and level of development.

24. Enjoyment of Learning and Bonding to School. Parents enjoy learning and express this through their own learning activities.

25. Reading for Pleasure. Parents read to toddlers every day and find ways for toddlers to participate in enjoyable reading experiences.

26. FAMILY VALUES CARING. Parents convey their beliefs about helping others by modeling their helping behaviors.

27. FAMILY VALUES EQUALITY AND SOCIAL JUSTICE. Parents place a high value on promoting social equality, religious tolerance, and reducing hunger and poverty while modeling these beliefs for children.

28. FAMILY VALUES INTEGRITY. Parents act on their convictions, stand up for their beliefs, and communicate and model this in the family.

29. FAMILY VALUES HONESTY. Parents tell the truth and convey their belief in honesty through their actions.

30. FAMILY VALUES RESPONSIBILITY. Parents accept and take personal responsibility.

31. FAMILY VALUES HEALTHY LIFESTYLE. Parents love children, setting the foundation for toddlers to develop healthy attitudes and beliefs about relationships. Parents model, monitor, and teach the importance of good health habits, and provide good nutritional choices and adequate rest and playtime.

32. PLANNING AND DECISION MAKING. Parents make all safety and care decisions for children and model safe behavior. As children become more

independently mobile, parents allow them to make simple choices.

33. INTERPERSONAL SKILLS. Parents model positive, constructive interactions with other people. Parents accept and are responsive to how toddlers use actions and words to express their feelings, seeing those expressions as cues to toddlers' needs.

34. CULTURAL COMPETENCE. Parents know and are comfortable with people of different cultural, racial, and/or ethnic backgrounds, and model this to children.

35. RESISTANCE SKILLS. Parents model resistance skills through their own behavior. Parents aren't overwhelmed by toddlers' needs and demonstrate appropriate resistance skills.

36. PEACEFUL CONFLICT RESOLUTION. Parents behave in acceptable, nonviolent ways and assist children in developing these skills by helping them solve problems when they're faced with challenging or frustrating circumstances.

37. PERSONAL POWER. Parents feel they have control over things that happen in their own lives and model coping skills, demonstrating healthy ways to deal with frustrations and challenges. Parents respond to

children so children begin to learn that they have influence over their immediate surroundings.

38. SELF-ESTEEM. Parents create an environment where children can develop positive self-esteem, giving children appropriate, positive feedback and reinforcement about their skills and competencies.

39. SENSE OF PURPOSE. Parents report that their lives have purpose and model these beliefs through their behaviors. Children are curious and explore the world around them.

40. POSITIVE VIEW OF PERSONAL FUTURE. Parents are hopeful and positive about their personal future and work to provide a positive future for children.

40 Assets PRESCHOOLERS
Need to Succeed
(Ages 3 to 5 Years)

1. FAMILY SUPPORT. Family life provides high levels of love and support.

2. POSITIVE FAMILY COMMUNICATION. Parents and pre-schoolers communicate positively. Preschoolers seek out parents for help with difficult tasks or situations.

3. OTHER ADULT RELATIONSHIPS. Preschoolers have support from at least one adult other than their

parents. Their parents have support from people outside the home.

4. CARING NEIGHBORHOOD. Children experience caring neighbors.

5. CARING OUT-OF-HOME CLIMATE. Children are in caring, encouraging environments outside the home.

6. PARENT INVOLVEMENT IN OUT-OF-HOME SITUATIONS. Parents are actively involved in helping preschoolers succeed in situations outside the home. Parents communicate preschoolers' needs to caretakers outside the home.

7. COMMUNITY VALUES CHILDREN. Parents and other adults in the community value and appreciate preschoolers.

8. CHILDREN ARE GIVEN USEFUL ROLES. Parents and other adults create ways preschoolers can help out and gradually include preschoolers in age-appropriate tasks.

9. SERVICE TO OTHERS. The family serves others in the community together.

10. SAFETY. Preschoolers have safe environments at home, in out-of-home settings, and in the neighborhood. This includes childproofing these environments.

11. FAMILY BOUNDARIES. The family has clear rules and consequences. The family monitors preschoolers and consistently demonstrates appropriate behavior through modeling and limit setting.

12. OUT-OF-HOME BOUNDARIES. Childcare settings and other out-of-home environments have clear rules and consequences to protect preschoolers while consistently providing appropriate stimulation and enough rest.

13. NEIGHBORHOOD BOUNDARIES. Neighbors take responsibility for monitoring and supervising children's behavior as they begin to play and interact outside the home.

14. ADULT ROLE MODELS. Parents and other adults model positive, responsible behavior.

15. POSITIVE PEER INTERACTION AND INFLUENCE. Preschoolers are encouraged to play and interact with other children in safe, well-supervised settings.

16. APPROPRIATE EXPECTATIONS FOR GROWTH. Adults have realistic expectations for children's development at this age. Parents, caregivers, and other adults encourage children to achieve and develop their unique talents.

17. CREATIVE ACTIVITIES. Preschoolers participate in music, art, dramatic play, or other creative activities each day.

18. OUT-OF-HOME ACTIVITIES. Preschoolers interact in stimulating ways with children outside the family. The family keeps preschoolers' needs in mind when attending events.

19. RELIGIOUS COMMUNITY. The family regularly attends religious programs or services while keeping children's needs in mind.

20. POSITIVE, SUPERVISED TIME AT HOME. Preschoolers are supervised by an adult at all times. Preschoolers spend most evenings and weekends at home with their parents in predictable, enjoyable routines.

21. ACHIEVEMENT EXPECTATION AND MOTIVATION. Parents and other adults convey and reinforce expectations to do well at work, at school, in the community, and within the family.

22. CHILDREN ARE ENGAGED IN LEARNING. Parents and family members model responsive and attentive attitudes at work, at school, in the community, and at home.

23. STIMULATING ACTIVITY AND HOMEWORK. Parents encourage children to explore and provide

stimulating toys that match children's emerging skills. Parents are sensitive to children's dispositions, preferences, and level of development.

24. ENJOYMENT OF LEARNING AND BONDING TO SCHOOL. Parents and other adults enjoy learning and engage preschoolers in learning activities.

25. READING FOR PLEASURE. Adults read to preschoolers for at least 30 minutes over the course of a day, encouraging preschoolers to participate.

26. FAMILY VALUES CARING. Preschoolers are encouraged to express sympathy for someone who is distressed and begin to develop a variety of helping behaviors.

27. FAMILY VALUES EQUALITY AND SOCIAL JUSTICE. Parents place a high value on promoting social equality, religious tolerance, and reducing hunger and poverty while modeling these beliefs for children.

28. FAMILY VALUES INTEGRITY. Parents act on their convictions, stand up for their beliefs, and communicate and model this in the family.

29. FAMILY VALUES HONESTY. Preschoolers learn the difference between telling the truth and lying.

30. Family Values Responsibility. Preschoolers learn that their actions affect other people.

31. Family Values Healthy Lifestyle. Parents and other adults model, monitor, and teach the importance of good health habits. Preschoolers begin to learn healthy sexual attitudes and beliefs as well as respect for others.

32. Planning and Decision Making. Preschoolers begin to make simple choices, solve simple problems, and develop simple plans at age-appropriate levels.

33. Interpersonal Skills. Preschoolers play and interact with other children and adults. They freely express their feelings and learn to put these feelings into words. Parents and other adults model and teach empathy.

34. Cultural Competence. Preschoolers are exposed in positive ways to information about and to people of different cultural, racial, and/or ethnic backgrounds.

35. Resistance Skills. Preschoolers are taught to resist participating in inappropriate or dangerous behavior.

36. PEACEFUL CONFLICT RESOLUTION. Parents and other adults model positive ways to resolve conflicts. Preschoolers are taught and begin to practice nonviolent, acceptable ways to deal with challenging and frustrating situations.

37. PERSONAL POWER. Parents feel they have control over things that happen in their own lives and model coping skills, demonstrating healthy ways to deal with frustrations and challenges. Parents respond to children so children begin to learn that they have influence over their immediate surroundings.

38. SELF-ESTEEM. Parents create an environment where children can develop positive self-esteem, giving children appropriate, positive feedback and reinforcement about their skills and competencies.

39. SENSE OF PURPOSE. Parents report that their lives have purpose and model these beliefs through their behaviors. Children are curious and explore the world around them.

40. POSITIVE VIEW OF PERSONAL FUTURE. Parents are hopeful and positive about their personal future and work to provide a positive future for children.

Subjects Index

Sources Index

A

Adamson, Crista, 267
Altman, Roberta, 268
American Academy of Pediatrics, 182, 301
American proverb, 227
Ames, Louis Bates, 187
Angelou, Maya, 57
Anonymous, 78, 172, 291, 312
Aquinas, Saint Thomas, 289
Ashe, Camera, 120

B

Bacall, Lauren, 145
Bailey, Pearl, 245
Barron-Tieger, Barbara, 147
Baum, L. Frank, 359
Becker, Gavin de, 104
Benin proverb, 3
Benson, Peter, 177, 250
Bernstein, Anne C., 167, 261
Big Bird, 161
Bismarck, Otto von, 170
Blair, Bonnie, 174
Blake, Bessie, 292
Boegehold, Betty, 175
Boetcker, William J. H., 10
Bombeck, Erma, 12
Bradley, Crenner, 42
Bradley, Tom, 49
Brazelton, T. Berry, 208, 365
Breathnach, Sara Ban, 253
Brecht, Bertolt, 72
Brenner, Barbara, 175
Brilliant, Ashleigh, 325
Brody, Jane, 26
Brown, Les, 204, 339
Buck, Pearl S., 76, 231
Buddha, 4

Buresh, Bernice, 354
Buscaglia, Leo, 211, 345
Bush, Barbara, 154
Butterworth, Robert, 105

C

Caddy, Eileen, 329
Cage, John, 110
Campbell, Joseph, 27, 37, 144
Canada, Geoffrey, 38
Carnegie Task Force on Learning, 133
Carroll, Lewis, 121, 271
Carson, Benjamin, 226
Castro, Susan, 79, 224, 298
Chávez, César, 126
Chief Dan George, 80
Chief Joseph, 313
Chinlund, Caroline, 60
Churchill, Winston, 143
Cicero, 73
Clarke, Jean Illsley, 297, 333
Clinton, Bill, 59
Clinton, Hillary Rodham, 258
Coleman, James, 160
Coles, Robert, 21, 83, 93, 229
Coloroso, Barbara, 84
Cosby, Bill, 265
Cree elder, 158
Crispell, Diane, 331
Csikszentmihalyi, Mihaly, 14, 316
Cudmore, L. L. Larison, 281

D

Davis, Adelle, 188
Day, Dorothy, 153
DeRienzo, Harold, 176
Didion, Joan, 137
Dinkmeyer, Don, 183
Disney, Walt, 152
Dockrey, Karen, 315
Dodge, Diane Trister, 101

Assets Index

About the Author

Jolene L. Roehlkepartain is a parent educator, author, and speaker on family and children's issues. She is a former magazine editor who launched two national magazines, *Adoptive Families* and *Children's Ministry.* She has worked with children through parks and recreation programs and congregational programs. She is the coauthor of *What Young Children Need to Succeed: Working Together to Build Assets from Birth to Age 11* and *A Leader's Guide to What Young Children Need to Succeed* (Free Spirit Publishing, 2000), which both won the 2000 Parent's Guide to Children's Media Award. Jolene is also the author of seventeen other books, including *Fidget Busters, Wiggle Tamers,* and *Building Assets Together,* and she is the coauthor of Search Institute's *Starting Out Right: Developmental Assets for Children.* She lives in Minneapolis with her husband and two children, ages four and ten.

Visit us on the Web!

www.freespirit.com

Stop by anytime to find our catalog with fast, easy, secure 24-hour online ordering; "Ask Our Authors," where visitors ask questions—and authors give answers—on topics important to children, teens, parents, teachers, and others who care about kids; links to other Web sites we know and recommend; fun stuff for everyone, including quick tips and strategies from our books; and much more! Plus our site is completely searchable so you can find what you need in a hurry. Stop in and let us know what you think!

Just point and click!

new! Get the first look at our books, catch the latest news from Free Spirit, and check out our site's newest features.

contact Do you have a question for us or for one of our authors? Send us an email. Whenever possible, you'll receive a response within 48 hours.

order! Order in confidence! Our secure server uses the most sophisticated online ordering technology available. And ordering online is just one of the ways to purchase our books: you can also order by phone, fax, or regular mail. No matter which method you choose, excellent service is our goal.

Win free books! As a way of thanking everyone who's made our Web site a success, we often have book giveaways online. Stop by and get in on the action!